Bimetallism: An Economic and Historical Analysis

This book presents a history of bimetallic monetary systems in Western economies and explains why bimetallic standards – rather than silver or gold standards – were in use from the time of Charlemagne until the nineteenth century. Professor Redish argues that token money was a necessary complement to a gold standard, but token money (a fortiori fiat money) needed technological and political expertise that were not in place until the nineteenth century. This book chronicles the difficulties of operating bimetallic standards, and the evolution of the technological and political prerequisites for the gold standard.

The simplicity of the gold standard, a monetary system where there is a fixed ratio between a weight of gold and a unit of currency, makes it an obvious focus for models of commodity money and for comparisons with today's fiat money systems. Yet, this book shows that to understand such critical features of the gold standard as its ability to credibly anchor the monetary system, it is necessary to understand how bimetallic standards worked.

Angela Redish is Professor of Economics at the University of British Columbia in Vancouver, British Columbia. She has been published in journals such as the *Journal of Economic History*, *Canadian Journal of Economics*, *Economic History Review*, *Explorations in Economic History*, *Journal of Monetary Economics*, *Financial History Review*, *Journal of Money, Credit and Banking* and *Oxford Economic Papers* and has also published many chapters in edited collections. Professor Redish is a member of the editorial board of the Studies in Macroeconomic History series published by Cambridge University Press.

STUDIES IN MACROECONOMIC HISTORY

Series Editor: Michael D. Bordo, *Rutgers University*

Editors:
Forrest Capie, *City University Business School*
Barry Eichengreen, *University of California, Berkeley*
Nick Crafts, *London School of Economics*
Angela Redish, *University of British Columbia*

The titles in this series investigate themes of interest to economists and economic historians in the rapidly developing field of macroeconomic history. The four areas covered include the application of monetary and finance theory, international economics, and quantitative methods to historical problems; the historical application of growth and development theory and theories of business fluctuations; the history of domestic and international monetary, financial, and other macroeconomic institutions; and the history of international monetary and financial systems. The series amalgamates the former Cambridge University Press series *Studies in Monetary and Financial History* and *Studies in Quantitative Economic History*.

Other books in the series:

Continued on page following index

Bimetallism: An Economic and Historical Analysis

ANGELA REDISH

University of British Columbia, Vancouver

PUBLISHED BY THE PRESS SYNDICATE OF THE UNIVERSITY OF CAMBRIDGE
The Pitt Building, Trumpington Street, Cambridge, United Kingdom

CAMBRIDGE UNIVERSITY PRESS
The Edinburgh Building, Cambridge CB2 2RU, UK   http//www.cup.cam.ac.uk
40 West 20th Street, New York, NY 10011-4211, USA   http//www.cup.org
10 Stamford Road, Oakleigh, Melbourne 3166, Australia
Ruiz de Alarcón 13, 28014 Madrid, Spain

First published 2000

Printed in the United States of America

Typeface Times 11/14 pt.   *System* QuarkXPress™   [BTS]

A catalog record for this book is available from the British Library.

Library of Congress Cataloging in Publication Data
Redish, Angela, 1952–
  Bimetallism : an economic and historical analysis / Angela Redish.
    p.   cm. – (Studies in macroeconomic history)
  Includes bibliographical references and index.
  ISBN 0-521-57091-3 (hb)
  1. Bimetallism.   2. Money – History.   3. Monetary policy.   I. Title.
II. Series.
HG562.R43   2000
332.4′23 – dc21   99-052882

ISBN   0 521 57091 3   hardback

To Anne and Ken Redish with thanks

Contents

ix

Acknowledgements

My interest in the operation of specie/commodity money regimes first emerged when Debbie Glassman and I tried to determine the money stock of France during the Price Revolution era. The issues that arose in our discussions have continued to intrigue me, leading me to ponder the monetary arrangements in the centuries before and after the early sixteenth century. So my first thanks go to Debbie for tangling with economic history.

That early fascination was fed by the support of an array of monetary historians. My friend Mike Bordo read and commented on the manuscript as well as the many papers that preceded it. Economists at the Federal Reserve Bank of Minneapolis, especially Warren Weber, have for the last fifteen years encouraged the quest to understand the operation of monetary regimes other than that of the second half of the twentieth century. Ann Carlos has read the manuscript and demonstrated her amazing ability to be simultaneously constructive and supportive. Of course none of them have responsibility for any errors.

The research underlying this book has been ongoing for

some fifteen years, during which time I have built up an impressive number of debts. I would like to thank the participants at seminars at the University of Toronto, McMaster University, Queens University, the University of Colorado, University of Western Ontario, Cornell, UCLA, University of Alberta, NBER and Federal Reserve Bank of Minneapolis.

Many of the ideas here have been developed in a series of articles: (1988), (with D. Glassman), "Currency Depreciation in Early Modern England and France," *Explorations in Economic History* 25: 75–97; (1990), "The Evolution of the Gold Standard in England," *Journal of Economic History*, 50(4): 789–805; (1993), "The Latin Monetary Union and the Emergence of the International Gold Standard" in M. Bordo and F. Capie, eds., *Monetary Regimes in Transition* (Cambridge), pp. 68–85; (1993), "Anchors Aweigh: The Transition from Commodity Money to Fiat Money in Western Economies," *Canadian Journal of Economics* 26: 777–95; and (1995), "The Persistence of Bimetallism in Nineteenth Century France," *Economic History Review* 48(4): 717–36.

This research was virtually all funded by a succession of SSHRCC research grants, and would not have been possible without them. I thank them. Finally for putting up with my absences and giving me joyful distractions I would like to thank Steve Elves and Jeff and Ben Hives.

1

From the Carolingian Penny to the Classical Gold Standard

For many economists the history of money begins with the classical gold standard and travels the century-long road to today's fiat money world. Questions of monetary regime focus on the contrast between the nominal anchor provided by the gold standard and the instability of the fiat money standard. In this view, under a gold standard the quantity of money, and hence the price level, is fixed by the quantity of gold or, more moderately, constrained by the rising cost of mining gold. In contrast, under a fiat money standard the monetary authorities can arbitrarily print money and may have an incentive to generate high rates of inflation.

But this simple dichotomy leaves important questions unanswered. The classical gold standard is typically dated from 1879 to 1914, and while numerous scholars have addressed why it was so short-lived by asking why it ended so soon, far fewer have questioned the initial date: why didn't the desire for a nominal anchor lead to a much earlier emergence of the gold standard?

An easy answer would be that the bimetallic standards that characterized Western economies for several centuries before the gold standard also provided a nominal anchor, because they too were commodity money regimes.[1] But this raises more questions than it answers, since bimetallic standards were not as stable as the short-lived gold standard, so the commodity nature of the gold standard may not have been the source of its stability. What then *was* the source of the stability? Why did the bimetallic standard evolve into the gold standard in the nineteenth century?

---

[1] See, for example, Bordo and Kydland (1995). In this book I use the term "commodity money" but essentially limit the discussion to the commodities of gold, silver and copper.

3

This study answers those questions and provides a framework for an integrated history of Western monetary regimes. I argue that prior to the nineteenth century two forces determined the characteristics of the monetary regime: the fiscal needs of the monetary authority and the need for a medium of exchange suitable for a wide range of transactions. The former imperative meant that debasement and depreciation were used when fiscal needs were urgent or alternative sources of financing were unavailable. As taxation methods and capital markets developed, the monetary authorities reduced their reliance on seignorage revenue.

The need for a medium of exchange led to the use of bimetallic standards – monetary regimes in which gold and silver coins were legal tender in a common unit of account – and the use of units of account. But as shown in Chapter 2, bimetallic standards exacerbated the inherent tendency for commodity money standards to depreciate over time. In the nineteenth century, technological change made possible the use of fiduciary monies such as token subsidiary coins and paper bank notes. Fiduciary money removed the necessity for bimetallism, and gradually the gold standard replaced bimetallic standards. The elimination of that source of currency instability coupled with the lack of a fiscal motive for depreciation led to the stability we now associate with the gold standard. The "nominal anchor" provided by the gold standard was not merely ordained by nature's endowment but required a social contract that governments would not use their power to generate seignorage revenue and a technology that made fiduciary monies feasible.

To set the stage for the study, I briefly review the evolution of European monetary standards from the penny standard of Charlemagne to the bimetallic standards of late medieval Europe. Charlemagne's monetary reform of 794 A.D. provides a natural starting point for the history of Western monetary standards. Charlemagne decreed that the money of the Holy Roman Empire should be the silver denarius, containing 1.7 grams of pure silver and weighing 1.9 grams.[2] While there were mints throughout the Empire, the dies from which the coins were stamped were all made centrally. Particularly at the fringes of the Empire where trade with the South and East were common, foreign gold coins were used in trade, including some gold coins minted under the late Roman Empire.

A system of counting emerged from two different sources: 12 denari were rated equal to 1 gold solidus – a Roman coin that had not been minted for two centuries but which still circulated; and, since 240 denari were cut from one pound weight of silver, 240 denari equalled one pound (£).[3] Thus arose the system where 240 denari (d) equalled 20 solidi (s) equalled £1. The important thing

[2] The weight of Charlemagne's denier is still disputed. Miskimin (1967) concludes that Charlemagne's reformed pound weight equalled 489 gms. and that the denier had 10% seignorage so that 264 were cut from 489 gms. of pure silver and each contained 1.85 gms. silver. Spufford (1988) bases his statement that the denier contained 1.7 gms. of silver on Grierson (1965). Bisson (1979: 5) states that the Carolingian seignorage rate was 4.5%. Note that when the medium of exchange and unit of account were identical, the rate of seignorage had to be the same as the alloy rate of the coin. This identity was not necessary once the unit of account and medium of exchange were separate.

[3] Although the name for the pound varied across states – *livre*, *libra* – the symbol £ was universal.

to note is that this was a system of counting (in dozens and scores of dozens) not a way of valuing alternative monies, and there were no coins representing either the pound or (for most of the period) the solidus. The quantity of money could be determined by counting ("telling") coins rather than by weighing silver. This distinction was critical but, at the time moot, since all coins had the same silver content.

However, this monetary regime did not remain in equilibrium. Two forces ended the "universal" money over the next four centuries. Firstly, and most simply, a significant portion of the coins wore away after decades of circulation and therefore newly minted pennies weighed more than older pennies. Secondly, the uniformity of the coinage declined with the waning power of the Holy Roman Empire. Coinage rights were gradually delegated to local abbots and counts who exploited the fact that coins were told rather than weighed, and profited by reducing the weight or fineness of the coins. By the end of the twelfth century the fineness of many of the deniers had been reduced to much less than 50 percent and the weight to about 1 gram. As a result, international and large-value transactions typically specified the type of the coin in which payments were to be made, implicitly generating a set of (flexible) exchange rates between coins or currencies.

Debasement and wear reduced the size and fineness of the pennies, but there were natural and social limits to this process. The social limits were incorporated in a series of contracts between citizens and monetary authorities and reflected the inefficiency of debasement as a tax. Citizens facilitated Pareto improvements whereby they agreed to pay alternative taxes in return for a commitment from the monetary authorities not to debase the money.

In a stagnant world, a return to Charlemagne's coinage might have been predicted, but political and economic systems had changed. The hegemony of the Holy Roman Empire had disappeared, so that responses to the monetary problems were at the state or city level and the gradual expansion of trade meant that the silver penny was not a convenient medium of exchange for all transactions. First in the Italian city states and then throughout Europe states introduced large silver coins and gold coins to complement the pennies and make a medium of exchange for high-value transactions.

The origin and nature of the "unit of account" – sometimes termed "ghost money" or "imaginary money" – was the subject of heated debate in the early twentieth century.[4] The synthesis of that debate by Marc Bloch (1954) suggested that the use of units of account evolved over the millennium.[5] He identifies three stages in the use of units of account. In the Carolingian era, as we have noted above, units of account were simply a system of counting and there were no coins representing the larger units. In the thirteenth to sixteenth centuries when the number of coins issued by a single monetary authority multiplied, the unit of account gradually became used to link the values of the various coins. The unit of account typically started out tied to a particular coin, say the denier, but over time, the denier might no longer be

---

[4] See Van Werveke (1934) and Einaudi (1953).

[5] Lane and Mueller (1985) apply this model in their masterful study of the early days of bimetallism in Venice.

minted, and the livre or pound became simply an abstract unit in which accounts were kept without any ties to a particular coin. For example, in France, the silver denier was last minted in 1519, but all coins were made legal tender in *livres tournois*, a unit based on the denier. This separation between the unit of account and the medium of exchange is Bloch's third stage in the evolution of units of account, which he dates roughly in the seventeenth century.

The separation of the unit of account and medium of exchange facilitated the depreciation of the currency. Depreciation is defined carefully below but essentially refers to a reduction in the specie (gold or silver) definition of the unit of account. With some very prominent exceptions, depreciation in England and France after the midfourteenth century occurred primarily in response to the physical limitations of bimetallic commodity standards and was not used expediently to generate revenue for the monetary authorities.

The book begins with an analysis of the constraints on commodity money standards. Examination of the methods by which commodity money standards could issue a range of denominations shows that each method had increasing costs as its range widened. Monetary authorities therefore adopted a combination of methods simultaneously, including bimetallism, trimetallism and the issue of low-fineness coins. I then argue that a variety of physical limitations of commodity money generated varying values of coins and precluded the "fixity" of value (1 unit of account = 1 unit of goods) that is touted as a principal advantage of commodity money. Finally, I argue that the stability of commodity money was not a time consistent policy. If agents expected stable money, the monetary authorities could gain, at least in the short run, by debasing or depreciating the currency.[6] Thus commodity money did not inherently provide the nominal anchor that is attributed to it.

Chapters 3 and 4 examine the monetary history of England and France in the context of the constraints on commodity money standards. Chapter 3 shows that in both countries the unit of account depreciated, so that bimetallic standards were not characterized by the stability associated with the classical gold standard. However, with the exception of a few spectacular episodes of debasement, the depreciation was not driven by fiscal objectives but by the objective of maintaining a circulation of coins trading at their legal tender value in the unit of account.

The problem of providing larger denomination coins was addressed throughout Western Europe by issuing large silver and gold coins; the problem of issuing smaller coins was not so easily resolved, and by the sixteenth century had become a major difficulty for monetary regimes. As noted above, no solution was perfect – coins of low fineness, trimetalllic (copper) coins and very small coins were all attempted, and Chapter 4 illustrates the experiments in England and France to resolve this.

Chapters 5–7 examine the transition from bimetallism to the gold standard in England, France and the United States. The transition occurred first in England and

---

[6] The term "monetary authorities" is used in discussions of contemporary monetary policy as it covers the gamut of government and semi-autonomous (e.g., central banks) organizations that determine policy. Here it is used similarly as an all-encompassing term for those who determine monetary policy, primarily kings, queens and parliaments.

involved a transition to a gold standard supplemented with fiduciary bank notes and small-denomination coins. The gold standard was a side-effect of the Industrial Revolution and emerged when technologies developed that could produce coins and notes that were not counterfeitable or at least were very costly to counterfeit.

The gold standard did create greater stability as changes in the relative price of gold to silver no longer induced responses of depreciation, but it is important to note that the "anchoring" of the monetary standard had emerged much earlier, and so in that sense the emergence of the gold standard was not a critical step in the creation of a nominal anchor.

Once the problem of issuing multiple denominations had been resolved, the focus of the debate about monetary standards became not how to provide a medium of exchange, but how to provide a stable price level.[7] This transition is clear in the history of choices over monetary regimes in France. In the late eighteenth century the revolutionary French government debated for fifteen years how to provide multiple denominations of currency and concluded by halfheartedly reverting to the bimetallic standard. Yet when the price of gold fell in the 1850s, the debate over the appropriate monetary standard

---

[7] Fetter (1965: 3) suggests similar timing: "I find practically no mention in any literature before 1797 of the idea that figured in discussions for a few years before and after the resumption of 1821, and was so prominent in the bimetallic controversy in the last quarter of the nineteenth century: that one metal would give more stable prices than would the other, or that the use of two metals as a standard would give greater price stability than would a single gold or silver standard".

contrasted a gold standard with fiduciary tokens with a renewed bimetallic standard, now promoted because it would enhance price stability. The de facto conclusion was in favour of the former, supported by the Latin Monetary Union, which created a currency union for fiduciary coins.

The histories of monetary standards of the United States and France are remarkably parallel. Both countries had revolutionary governments at the end of the eighteenth century that decimalized the monetary standard but retained bimetallism, and both countries abandoned bimetallism de facto in the 1850s following the gold discoveries. Finally both ended the free (i.e., unlimited) coinage of silver in the 1870s in ways that reflected their recent wartime experiences. That said, there were differences: the United States adopted a bimetallic standard after the American Revolution with very little debate, in contrast to the long and deep debate in France; the Americans responded to the de facto silver standard of the 1830s by decreasing the gold content of the dollar in 1834, while the French did not respond; finally, while both the Franco-Prussian War and the U.S. Civil War affected the transition to the gold standard, they did so in very different ways. The Civil War had led to a paper money standard under which the end of free silver coinage in the United States, the so-called Crime of 1873, was not so noticeable; the Franco-Prussian war had enriched Germany, and as Germany used its wealth to join the gold standard, the French government acted to prevent being the recipient of Germany's unwanted silver.

The technology of producing coins in a variety of denominations is an important explanatory variable for the evolution from the penny standard to the classical gold standard. Yet the gold standard – typically supplemented by convertible privately issued bank notes and government-issued low-denomination coins – that had solved the denomination problem, quickly evolved into a fiat money regime. The concluding chapter argues that the qualities required by a monometallic monetary standard complemented by a range of denominations provided by fiduciary money were the same as those required for fiat money – uncounterfeitable money issued by a credible monetary authority. Fiat money then presented the logical culmination of the gradual weakening of the commodity link under a fiduciary money standard.

There is a large gap between the economics literature on the commodity money standard and the historical literature. To economists, commodity money is a sparse construct, a simple way of tying down the monetary side of the economy. In contrast, historians have filled vast tomes with details of the characteristics and operation of commodity money standards – to them commodity money is a complex beast. This book attempts to straddle the gap between these two literatures, to allow for a more complex monetary system than the economists' "commodity money" and to find generalities that are buried in the historians' details.

2

The Mechanics of
Commodity Money

Mechanics of Commodity Money

This chapter suggests three propositions that relate to the evolution of Western monetary standards. They are presented in a rather abstract fashion here, and in the following chapters I document how they influenced the history of monetary regimes in the Western world. The first proposition is that commodity money regimes could not easily (i.e., costlessly) provide a range of denominations. The second proposition argues that the use of multiple coins with fixed values in a common unit of account to solve the denomination problem significantly exacerbated the potential for undervaluation of coins, leading to an inherent tendency for the unit of account to depreciate over time. Finally, I argue that commodity money standards faced problems of time consistency of optimal policy similar to those facing fiat money regimes. None of these propositions is straightforward, and together they illustrate the complexity of commodity money regimes.

THE NEED FOR MULTIPLE DENOMINATIONS

As markets developed, the need for a medium of exchange developed into the need for *multiple* media of exchange. Small-scale transactions needed low-value coins, while higher scale transactions needed a higher value medium of exchange. The problem then was how to provide these multiple media. Figure 2.1 illustrates the alternative ways in which multiple media of exchange could be provided. Most modern economies have solved the denomination problem by issuing fiat monies – definitionally, monies that

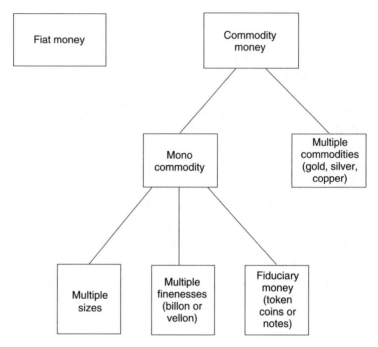

Figure 2.1. Monetary standards providing multiple denominations.

are intrinsically useless and inconvertible – which can readily be issued in a variety of denominations.

Commodity money regimes addressed the need for a range of denominations either by issuing coins in metals of varying values, most typically in some combination of gold, silver and copper, or by one of the three types of monometallic standard. Consider a silver standard: multiple denominations can be created (1) by issuing pure silver coins in a wide variety of sizes, (2) by issuing coins in a variety of finenesses[1] or (3) by supplementing a basic single denomination coin with fiduciary monies convertible into those silver coins. Methods (1) and (2) entail the issue of full-bodied coins, that is, coins which circulate at values close to their intrinsic value. In contrast, fiduciary coins circulate at a value greater than their intrinsic value.

Sargent and Velde (1998) have argued that a commodity money regime in which the market issues coins on demand (bimetallic or monometallic) will be unable to provide stable full-bodied coinages in different denominations. They build a model of market provision of multiple denominations of silver coinage which captures many characteristics of the medieval/early modern European monetary environment: shortages of small coins, large-denomination coins trading at premia and the gradual debasement of the currency. They show that where two coins are freely minted and sold at the price of their metal (intrinsic value) plus costs of production, there cannot be sustained coexistence of both coins in the face of price fluctuations, when their production costs differ. Sargent and Velde's result implies that sustained coexistence of, for example, a large silver coin which was cheap to produce relative to its value and a small, therefore costly to produce, silver coin, would not be feasible. In the model, relative to an initial equilibrium in which agents use both large and small coins, a small increase in income increases the demand for pennies (small coins) and dollars (large

---

[1] The fineness of a coin refers to its purity, that is, the percentage of alloy.

17

coins) but there exists an equilibrium where the agents are content not to buy pennies because dollars are expected to appreciate, and so they are unwilling to sell dollars to the mint to buy pennies, a situation defined as a small coin shortage.[2]

As we shall see in Chapters 3 and 4, these supply problems were significant constraints on the issue of multiple denominations of commodity money in England and France. The remainder of this section considers other difficulties implied by the issue of multiple denominations in a commodity money regime. In the following chapters, I examine how the monetary authorities in England and France varied their choices from this menu of alternatives as technologies and political constraints changed.

Varying Sizes

The problem of multiple monies is motivated by the constraints on the convenient size of a coin. Jevons suggested (1899: 153) that "Coins must not be so small that they can be easily lost, or can with difficulty be picked up. The rule seems to be that the coin should cover the whole area of

---

[2] Sustained coexistence would be feasible if the production of the larger coin were taxed, that is, if there were a seignorage charge on the larger coin equal to the difference in production costs. However, such a seignorage charge might make the coin profitable to replicate, encouraging counterfeiting. Furthermore, the optimal seignorage charge was lower on higher value coins because they could be supplied by foreign mints, while the small-denomination coinage was usually dominated by domestic coins. If a large seignorage charge were placed on the larger silver coins, silver would be taken to foreign mints for coining.

contact between the points of the thumb and first finger". In his seventeenth-century treatise on monetary policy, Bodin (1606: 689) recommended minting coins of 16, 32 and 64 per mark (3.8 gms., 7.5 gms. and 15 gms., respectively). He argued that coins that were smaller than 1.3 grams were difficult to stamp, and too brittle, while coins that were larger than 31 grams were easy to counterfeit.[3] These broader limits would make possible a range of values of $1:24$ in a homogeneous commodity. As economies developed therefore, silver – an object of intermediate value – was too valuable to provide a medium of exchange for the smallest transactions and too cheap to use for high-value transactions.

A North American dime weighs about 2.25 grams. Table 2.1 presents some data on wage rates in England and France and relates those wage rates to the weight of silver they represented, which varied between about 3 and 6.5 grams per day. Thus, a coin the size of a dime would be worth from a quarter of a day's work to about 70 percent of a day's work in early modern France. In England it would be about 70% of a day's work throughout the period. That is, if a coin the size of a dime were the smallest available coin, it would be equivalent in 1999 to the smallest unit of the medium of exchange being worth

---

[3] He is not more precise. The counterfeiting could have been through filling the interior of a coin. In the 1860s the U.S. Mint became concerned that it was profitable to replace the gold interior of the "double eagle" (516 grs., 33 gms.) with platinum (Jevons, 1899: 157). The main deterrent to this practice was the high density of gold, which made cheap "fillings" obvious. Similarly Dumas (1868: 92) notes that 100 franc and 50 franc coins were rarely used as they were liable to be altered by filling the middle with lead.

19

Table 2.1. *Weight of Silver per Day's Work*

a. France

	Wages	Coin	Grams of Silver
1400	2.5st	gros – 1st; 2.55 gms.	5.1
1500	2.5st	gros – 3st; 3.4 gms.	2.83
1600	10st	teston – 14/6st; 9.6 gms.	6.62
1700	17st	quarts d'écu – 18st; 6.85 gms.	6.47

b. England

	Wages	Coin	Grams of Silver
1400	3.5d	penny – 1d; 1.18 gms.	4.14
1500	4d	penny – 1d; 0.79 gms.	3.16
1600	8d	penny – 1d; 0.52 gms.	4.16
1700	13d	penny – 1d; 0.51 gms.	6.52

Note: English wages are in pence sterling (d) and French wages are in sols tournois (st). Note that 1 troy grain is 0.0648 gms.; 1 marc silver is 244.7569 gms. silver. Tables 2.1a and 2.1b are inconsistent in that the English coins are composed of sterling silver (0.91666% fine) while the French coins are 0.898% fine silver (0.9375 fine *argent-le-roi*).

Sources: Wages for both France and England are daily wages for building labourers: England (Brown and Hopkins); France (Baulant); coins: England (Challis); France (de Wailly).

(assuming a wage of about $5/hour or $40 per day) from $10 to $28!

If only silver coins were minted, however, they would be very cumbersome for mercantile trade. Gold coins – being between ten and sixteen times more valuable than silver by weight (more by volume due to gold's greater density) – implied a much lower transactions cost for large payments.

Varying Finenesses

The inconvenient link between coin size and coin value could be broken by issuing coins of varying fineness. An alloy of silver and copper could be used to produce coins of a lower value than pure silver coins of the same size and higher value than copper coins of the same size. In France coins of this alloy were called "billon," in Spain, "vellon."[4] Similarly, an alloy of gold with copper or silver could produce low-denomination coins of reasonable size, obviating the need for a bimetallic regime. But such low-fineness coins were not feasible for a variety of metallurgical reasons.

Counterfeiting would be profitable if it were impossible, or at least very costly, to distinguish between a coin with 5% gold and 95% copper (or silver) and one with 2% gold and 98% copper. This was in fact the case, and the primary rationale for not using alloyed metals for coining was the need to be able to determine the fineness of coins relatively easily. Craig (1953: 103) describes the optimal fineness for coining as follows: "Fine gold is too soft and malleable to wear well. The design can even be obliterated without actual abrasion by flow of metal. On the other hand, an addition of alloy beyond an 11th or 12th, unless it is such a balanced medley of metals as impedes easy verification, spoils the colour and aids the counterfeiter". Similarly, Harris (1757: 508) in his eighteenth-century treatise on coins considered the possi-

---

[4] For obvious reasons, if the silver content were low the coins were called black money, whereas billon coins with greater than 50% silver were called white money.

bility of issuing "base" money to provide small-denomination coins in England:[5]

> When the standard of fineness is much baser than ours is at present, different degrees of deviations from it are not conspicuous to the eye; and the precise fineness cannot be so well ascertained, even by skilful assay-masters. By this scheme of coining base money, besides furnishing opportunities to counterfeiters amongst ourselves, we should lay a temptation in the way of foreigners, to commit the same frauds.

The cheapest and most common method of assaying was to use a touchstone, which is estimated to have had an accuracy of ± 2–3% in the early modern period, and perhaps ± 1% in the nineteenth century.[6] The touchstone was typically made of a smooth, hard, dark basaltic rock, like a black marble. It would be used in two stages. Firstly an alloy to be tested was scraped over the stone and the assayer compared the streak left with that made by a touch needle (see Illustration 2.1). Each assayer had several sets of needles, whose tips were of gold and silver of varying known degrees of fineness. For example, Cramer

---

[5] Vaughan (1675: 31), writing one hundred years earlier, notes that low-fineness coins would be a way to create a large-size, small-denomination coin but that the inconvenience outweighs the benefit: "by this mixture both the colour, sound, weight and the other more hidden qualities of the different metals, are so confounded as the falsity cannot be discovered but with extream difficulty. . . . In all those countries where base money hath course, the greatest part of it is not coyned by the state".   [6] Moore and Oddy (1985: 59).

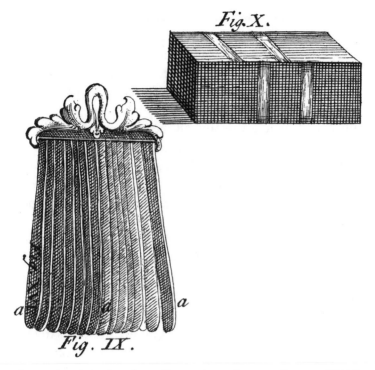

Illustration 2.1. Touchneedles and touchstone. Cramer (1741). Courtesy of Woodward Library, University of British Columbia.

recommended that an assayer have four sets of gold needles and one set of silver needles.[7] The gold needles declined by half-carat finenesses from 24c to 20c and then by 1 carat because the touchstone could not distinguish

---

[7] The silver set would have sixteen needles varying from pure silver to 1/16th silver and 15/16 copper. Four sets of gold needles were needed to reflect the possible combinations of copper and silver in the alloy: pure copper, pure silver, equal parts copper and silver, and 2 : 1 copper to silver.

23

more finely at lower finenesses. (Ercker, 1686, recommended gold needles down to 12 carats only.)

To ensure that the colour on the touchstone streak was truly obtained from gold or silver, an assayer would drop acid on the streaks (aqua fortis for gold-coloured streaks, and aqua regia for silver). The aqua fortis (nitric acid) would dissolve all metals but gold, and aqua regia (nitric acid and hydrochloric acid) would dissolve gold. Thus assayers dissolved any admixture of base metals such as tin, arsenic and zinc which might have given false colour (Cramer, 1741). The advantage of the touchstone, for example over assays that essentially involved refining the metal, was that it left the coin whole, and was cheap and quick. However, the disadvantage was that it could not distinguish very easily between metals of low fineness.

Other characteristics of alloyed metals also promoted the use of fine gold and silver for coining. For coins to have a market value close to their costs of production, it was necessary to be able to extract the specie metal (gold or silver) relatively easily; yet as the proportion of specie fell, the costs of refining rose.[8] In addition, it was necessary that the alloy be homogeneous; that is, when the alloy was rolled out all coins were required to have the same fineness. It was not enough that the bar have on average a given fineness; rather every small piece of the bar had to have that exact fineness. Low-fineness alloys did not have this uniformity.

---

[8] Vaughan (1675: 33) suggests that a base money penny containing a "penny" worth of silver trades at a discount to its pure metal content "because the mixture makes that you cannot extract this penny in pure metal without loss and charge".

Fiduciary Money

The last monometallic option to consider is the issue of fiduciary monies that are convertible into, for example, silver coins. Such fiduciary monies include convertible bank notes and token coins and could be issued by private or public institutions. The most common were large-denomination, privately issued bank notes and small-denomination, publicly issued token coins. The key difficulties faced by issuers of fiduciary money (and a fortiori fiat money) are counterfeiting and credibility. Counterfeiting, specifically replicating the fiduciary money, is profitable because by definition the money can be converted into goods with a higher intrinsic value. Credibility matters because, if the guarantee of convertibility is not trusted, the coin/note will either depreciate to its intrinsic value or (possibly) circulate as a fiat money. These impediments sharply limited the issue of fiduciary monies and led to the adoption of bimetallic and sometimes trimetallic monetary systems, despite the problems inherent in such monetary standards.

The returns to counterfeiting a given note or coin increase with denomination, but the costs to an individual of accepting a bogus money also increase with denomination. The Bank of England began issuing notes in 1696, but the first notes were handwritten and the history of its note issues is of partially successful attempts to stay one step ahead of the counterfeiters and to have the government enforce and increase punishments for counterfeiters. The primary rationale for the issue of only large denominations of notes (£25 and higher) was that individuals would have an incentive to inspect such notes very carefully. At the other end of the spectrum, the returns to counterfeiting low-value coins were small, but the incentive to inspect the coins was also smaller.

Multiple Commodities

Within a commodity money regime, the alternative to monometallic standards is multicommodity money standards. The most common standards used in the West were gold and silver, gold and copper or silver and copper. Multiple commodity standards could produce coins in a range of values, without the problems identified for monometallic systems. The only drawback, and it was a very significant one, was the difficulty of maintaining a constant relationship between coins in two (or more) different metals when their relative market prices could, and did, vary. The problems of undervaluation inherent to multimetallic standards are described in the following section; here I will simply note that the problems increased dramatically with the number of commodities assigned a monetary role.

In summary, using varying sizes or finenesses of coins, issuing fiduciary money and using multiple commodities could all reduce the denomination problem, but each implied costs, and the costs rose with the span of values (denominations) covered. For example, a coin that was fiduciary but whose intrinsic value was 90% of its official value would yield a smaller incentive to counterfeiters than one whose intrinsic value was 10% of its official value. The economist would therefore predict that an optimizing monetary authority would use each method to some extent (i.e., to the extent that equalised marginal costs). As we shall see, this is precisely what occurred.

UNDERVALUATION AS A CAUSE OF DEPRECIATION

In the monetary systems of Western Europe, the minting of coins was basically market driven. Coinage was "free" in the sense that anyone could bring metal to the mint for coining – at a price.[9] The monetary authority posted a mint price (MP), measured in units of account, for a given weight of silver or gold of a particular fineness, and then coined the metal brought in. The mint price would be paid in coins whose legal tender value equalled the mint price. If we define the mint equivalent (ME) as the legal tender value of coins made from that weight of metal, then the nominal gross profit or seignorage per unit weight of gold or silver is the difference between the mint equivalent and mint price.[10]

For example, in England in 1615 the unit of account was the pound sterling, comprising twenty shillings (20/–), each of twelve pence (12d). The law provided for the coinage of "unites" weighing 140.8 troy grains of gold 91.67% fine,

[9] Free coinage refers to the mint being required to buy metal from all sellers, not to gratuitous minting. See below.

[10] Boizard (1696) refers to this combination of pure profit and brassage (or costs) as "rendage". While it is convenient to have a distinct word for this term, I will follow the literature in using "gross seignorage" for the sum and "net seignorage" for the pure profit of the mint.

and made them legal tender for 20/– (20 shillings stg.), implying a mint equivalent 74.4 shillings per ounce.[11] The mint price of gold was 72 shillings per ounce so that the gross seignorage was 2.4 shillings or 3% of ME_g. Since the mint paid for metal it purchased in coins made from that metal, a useful way to think about the gross seignorage rate is as a processing fee for minting.

The mint equivalent is definitionally the value of a coin divided by the product of its fineness and its weight, but the mint equivalent was not announced to the public; they were only informed of the name of the coin ("unite" in the preceding example) and its value (20 shillings in the example). The fineness and weight had to be inferred or anticipated.

If there were multiple media of exchange, agents receiving payments for debts or goods denominated in the unit of account would receive the greatest quantity of specie (that is, pure gold or silver) if they were paid in coins with the lowest mint equivalent. I will define a coin as undervalued if it has a mint equivalent lower than that of another circulating coin. In a mono-coin standard the leading causes of undervaluation were wear from circulation and clipping. Jevons (1899: 156) noted that an English sovereign would lose about 1% of its weight in twenty years, while it would take only ten years for a half-sovereign.[12] Thus newly minted coins were undervalued relative to the coins that had been in circulation. In 1798 it was found that the crowns in circulation were 3.3% light,

---

[11] 1 Troy ounce contained 480 grains, so that $ME_g = 20/[(140.8/480) *.9167] = 74.4$.

[12] See also Patterson (1972: 220) and Mayhew (1974: 3).

and the shillings 25% lighter than at issue. The other major source of undervaluation was the operation of "clippers" who, particularly prior to the seventeenth century, profited from the heterogeneity of newly minted coins by clipping a small amount of metal from relatively large coins rendering them overvalued relative to full-weight coins.

While undervaluation could occur under a monometallic standard, it was even more of a problem for bimetallic standards. Under a bimetallic standard coins of two metals are given legal tender values in the unit of account. English practice in the early seventeenth century illustrates the generic problem. In England in 1615 the silver "sixpence" was legal tender in addition to the gold unite. The sixpence was 11/12 pure (or fine) silver, weighed 46.8 (troy) grains, and was valued at 6 pence so that its mint equivalent was 67.13d (or 5.6 shillings) per ounce troy of fine silver.[13] The mint bought silver at 64.91d per troy ounce, so the gross seignorage was 2.22d per ounce. The ratio of the mint equivalents of gold and silver embodied in the coinage was 13.3 (74.4/5.6).

Assume that there is a large world bullion market in which the relative price of gold to silver is R.[14] If the ratio R exceeded 13.3 in 1615, then the mint undervalued gold (overvalued silver), and if $R < 13.3$, then the mint overvalued gold (undervalued silver). Since the relative market price of gold to silver varied over

---

[13] Value in shillings divided by product of the weight in ounces and the fineness: $(.5/[(46.8/480)*.917])$.

[14] This simplifying assumption obviates the need for dealing explicitly with mint prices and mint equivalents in other countries and implicitly assumes that the foreign buying and selling prices of gold and silver are the same.

time, even if the monetary authorities chose the mint equivalents so as to avoid undervaluing either metal at the date the coins were valued, the market price ratio would invariably deviate from the ratio of mint equivalents over time, causing one of the metals to become undervalued.

The effects of undervaluation have been very hotly debated by economists throughout time, in a debate that we can call the Gresham's Law debate. Undervalued money is "good" money, overvalued money is "bad" money and according to Gresham's Law, "Bad money drives out good". Yet a variety of other consequences of undervaluation were possible. Good money might circulate at a premium (that is, at its market value) or it might even circulate at par.

We begin by examining the rationale and necessary conditions for Gresham's Law. Suppose that there are old and newly minted gold coins, and that the old coins contained less gold than newly minted ones. If both coins were accepted for domestic debts (or goods) at the same value, then agents would pay those debts with their old rather than their new (heavier) coins. The good money would be used to pay international debts (on the assumption that internationally the coins were valued by their intrinsic value) or melted down. Thus bad money would circulate domestically and good money would eventually be driven out of domestic circulation.

The speed with which Gresham's Law is predicted to act depended upon the degree of undervaluation. Consider a bimetallic standard: if the relative mint equivalents were slightly (to be defined below) different from the market price ratio, there would be a tendency for the currency to degenerate toward monometallism. For example, if gold was undervalued (that is, $R > [\mathrm{ME}_g/\mathrm{ME}_s]$) it would be exported in years of balance-of-payments surplus, while silver would be imported in years of balance-of-payments deficits. The progression toward monometallism would typically take a number of years as the size of balance-of-payments deficits and surpluses was small relative to the money stock.

If, on the other hand, coin ratings were more than slightly incorrect, bimetallic arbitrage – the export of one metal to import the other – would be profitable and the currency would very quickly degenerate into monometallism. If we ignore temporarily transaction costs other than domestic minting fees, it would be profitable to export 1 ounce of gold to import R ounces of silver (for sale to the mint) if R times the mint price of silver exceeded the mint equivalent of gold ($\mathrm{ME}_g < R \cdot \mathrm{MP}_s$). Similarly, the export of silver for gold would be profitable if the mint price of gold divided by R exceeded the mint equivalent of silver ($\mathrm{ME}_s < (1/R) \cdot \mathrm{MP}_g$). Using the relationship ME_i equals MP_i plus s_i, bilateral arbitrage would be profitable if

$$\mathrm{ME}_s < \frac{\mathrm{ME}_g - s_g}{R} \quad \text{or} \quad \mathrm{ME}_s > \frac{\mathrm{ME}_g}{R} + s_s$$

That is, if the mint equivalent of silver were low enough to cover the seignorage, it would pay to export silver coins and import gold for sale to the mint. Alternatively, if the mint equivalent of silver were sufficiently high, it would be profitable to export gold and import silver. Transactions

31

costs expand the range within which an incorrect rating would not lead to bimetallic arbitrage.[15]

Given the assumption of circulation at par or by tale, the "driving out" of good money seems unexceptional, but (1) the assumption is not obviously justified and (2) the result is a partial equilibrium not a general equilibrium result.

Although Galbraith (1975: 10) suggested that Gresham's Law "is perhaps the only economic law that has never been challenged", in fact it has been disputed by many economists in this century, and possibly others earlier.[16] Rolnick and Weber (1986) reopened the Gresham's Law debate arguing that Gresham's Law should be rejected on both empirical and theoretical grounds for all but small-denomination coins. They

---

[15] If transactions costs are incorporated the conditions are slightly more complex. Let d_i, where i equals silver or gold, represent transaction costs (in domestic unit of account per ounce) of exporting or importing gold and silver, respectively. These costs include transportation, insurance, interest on metal at the mint waiting to be coined, commissions, and so forth. Arbitrageurs would export gold if ME_g plus d_g plus R times d_s were less than R times MP_s and would export silver if ME_s times R plus d_s times R plus d_g were less than MP_g. Thus bimetallic arbitrage would be profitable if,

$$ME_s < \frac{ME_g - s_g}{R} - \left[d_s + \frac{d_g}{R}\right] \quad \text{or} \quad ME_s > \frac{ME_g}{R} + s_s + \left[d_s + \frac{d_g}{R}\right]$$

[16] Hawtrey (1923: 204) stated that "it must not be supposed that the law [Gresham's] is true without exception or qualification" and used as an example the circulation of guineas at a premium in seventeenth-century England because the use of silver would have been "intolerably inconvenient". See also, Fetter (1931) and Miskimin (1972).

suggested that undervalued coins would circulate at a market premium equal to the degree of undervaluation and would not be driven from circulation. In support of this assertion they noted that there were several historical instances of coins circulating at a premium. Furthermore, they noted that Gresham's Law would predict that there would be no coinage of undervalued metals, while in the early nineteenth century gold coins were minted in the United States, although gold was undervalued at the U.S. Mint.

Sargent and Smith (1997) use circulation by tale as a maintained hypothesis, and examine whether Gresham's Law holds in a general equilibrium environment. They use a cash in advance constraint model in a world where coins can lose weight through wear, to observe whether the "good" money will circulate at par, at a premium or not at all. Perhaps unsurprisingly given the fixed supply of the overvalued (i.e., worn) coins, the answer can be either positive or negative depending on parameters in the model.

The following chapters discuss the effect of undervaluation extensively and find the evidence ambiguous. But, as we will see, the response of the monetary authorities to undervaluation is not ambiguous. They depreciated the coinage, or in other words, increased the mint equivalent of the new coins. Note that undervaluation in a bimetallic standard could be removed either by depreciating the undervalued metal or by appreciating the overvalued metal. Yet in virtually all instances it was the former that occurred.[17]

---

[17] Where undervaluation occurred because of clipping or wear, there was also the possibility of either maintaining the specie value of the unit of account, in which case the loss of metal would have to be paid

The depreciation could take the form of enhancing the money (defined as raising the legal tender value of a coin) or a debasement (lowering the weight or fineness of a coin). For large-denomination coins it usually occurred through the former, while for small-denomination coins, for which a 10% rise would not yield an aliquot denomination, it occurred through debasement, usually accomplished by reducing the weight of the coin. After a certain point a new large coin would be introduced, and the whole process would start over again.

DEPRECIATION AS A REVENUE SOURCE

Undervaluation is one explanation for depreciation of the coinage, a second is the use of debasement or inflation to raise revenue for the monetary authority, typically the monarch. It is useful to break down the profit opportunities into the equilibrium opportunity and "cheating". The former is simply the net seignorage described above, and we can build a simple static model of the behavior of a revenue-maximising monetary authority by assuming that the monetary authority chooses a seignorage rate (or equivalently mint price) that maximizes seignorage revenue, conditional on an exogenously given mint equivalent and a demand for coins that would depend on many factors, but not least on the seignorage rate.[18] The usual

for by either coin holders or government, or by depreciating the coinage. The English recoinage of 1696 reflected one of the very rare instances where the former occurred; see Chapter 5.

[18] Here I am ignoring the distinction between gross and net seignorage, implicitly assuming that the brassage rate is constant.

result holds that to maximise seignorage, the monetary authorities would set the seignorage rate such that the elasticity of demand for mint output with respect to the profit rate equalled -1.[19] The optimal seignorage rate would then depend on the elasticity of output with respect to the profit rate, and the less elastic the demand for coins the higher the revenue-maximising seignorage rate.

In Chapter 3, I argue that this simple model can explain differences in seignorage rates across metals, countries and time during much of the bimetallic period. The demand for coins is quite elastic, and optimal steady-state seignorage rates appear to be considerably less than 10 percent through most of the period. However, during much of the medieval period, and occasionally in the early modern period, there were "debasement" periods when seignorage rates were far higher than this model can explain. The problem is that the simple model assumes that agents can accurately gauge the mint equivalent of coins, and it does not allow the monetary authority to "cheat". If it were possible to "fool" people then the monetary authorities could make greater profits, although when the unit of account and medium of exchange were tied, as under Charlemagne's penny standard, the potential gains were limited. The monetary authority could debase the coinage (defined as a reduction in the weight or fineness of a coin) and if agents did not realize what had happened, the mint would make greater seignorage than before, without

---

[19] The aggregate (gross) seignorage per period was the product of the quantity of output (Q) and the (gross) seignorage rate (ρ). Aggregate gross profits are given by $\rho\,Q(\rho)$ and to maximize profits we take the derivative of $\rho * Q(\rho)$ with respect to ρ and set it equal to zero yielding the condition that $Q'(\rho) \cdot \rho / Q = -1$.

Table 2.2. *Profits from Debasement: An Example*

Line	Weight (grs.)	Fineness	Gold Content (grains)	Value of Coin (shillings)	Mint Equivalent (shillings per oz.)	Mint Price (shillings per oz.)	Profit (shillings per oz.)
A	140.8	22c	129.07	20/–	74.4	72	2.4
B	140.8	20c	117.33	20/–	81.8	73	8.8
C	140.8	22c	129.07	21/–	78.1	75.7	2.4

affecting the flow of metal to the mint (since the expected seignorage rate had not changed).

Returning to the example of the "unite" above (ignore the issue of wear for the moment) suppose that the monetary authority raised the mint price to 73 shillings without announcing a change in the value of unites. This would appear to reduce the seignorage rate and would therefore encourage the sale of metal to the mint.[20] However, if the monetary authority had raised the mint equivalent surreptitiously by lowering the weight or fineness of the unite, then they could increase the seignorage rate and the flow of metal to the mint simultaneously. For example, if the fineness were reduced from 22 carat to 20 carat, then the mint equivalent would be 81.84 shillings, and the new seignorage rate 12 percent (see line B, Table 2.2).

This gain would be a transitory phenomenon as agents would eventually notice the lower gold content of the unite, depending on how aggressively the coin had been

[20] If we assume that agents thought that the monetary authority was maximizing net seignorage, and that therefore the previous rate was revenue maximizing, we need to assume that they allow for the possibility for the demand for coins to have shifted, lowering the optimal seignorage rate.

debased. In addition to being transitory, the gains were also limited by the initial gold content of the unite. Note that in this example, the official value of the unite was not changed, implying that (1) the debasement would not be immediately obvious and (2) the debasement profits did not depend on the assumption that the unit of account and the medium of exchange were separate.[21]

If the unit of account and medium of exchange were separated, the monetary authorities had an alternative policy that could generate profits even if it were observed. Suppose that the monetary authority openly depreciated the unite raising its legal tender value to 21 shillings, and raised the mint price to 75.7 shillings (see line C, Table 2.2). The seignorage rate is still at its revenue-maximising level (2.4 shillings/oz.). However, since the new mint price is higher than the mint equivalent of the old unites (74.4 shillings/oz.), agents would be better off bringing their old unites to the mint, where they receive 75.7 shillings for coins containing an ounce of pure gold, than if they used them for debts or purchases, when the same weight of coins would only be accepted for 74.4 shillings. Thus the monetary authorities have increased revenues above their equilibrium maximum. (While the two tools of debasement and a "reminting" depreciation have been discussed separately to clarify each process, they could have been and, as shown in Chapter 3, were used simultaneously.)

---

[21] In Chapter 3 I argue that monetary authorities could benefit from debasing the denier even when there was no separation between the unit of account and the medium of exchange, although the debasement revenues were less than in the early modern period when the unit of account and medium of exchange were distinct.

The ability to raise seignorage in this way depended on whether or not coins traded by their legal tender value, as well as on the ability of the monetary authority to "fool" the agents bringing money to the mint. For a debasement the "fooling" required that agents not anticipate that the mint price would be paid in debased coins; for a "reminting depreciation" the fooling required that agents prior to the depreciation did not anticipate a depreciation as then they would have benefitted from waiting to sell gold to the mint. If we assume for the moment that such "fooling" was possible, then the optimal monetary policy was not time consistent.[22] That is, the monetary authorities could tell agents that they would not debase the coins, and if the public believed them, the optimal policy for the authorities would be to debase the coins. In this environment, the equilibrium that would be observed if agents did not trust the authorities would depend on the costs to the authorities of debasement. If debasing imposed costs on the monetary authorities, then agents would not expect them to raise the rate of debasement above the "break-even" point.

This "discretionary" equilibrium would be worse for both parties than the equilibrium that would result if the monetary authorities could "credibly commit" not to debase or depreciate. This problem was sometimes solved in medieval times by the agents agreeing to pay a tax conditional on the monetary authorities not debasing the coinage. In general, however, solutions to the commitment problem have been difficult to identify theoretically or

---

[22] What follows builds on the extensive literature that followed the work of Kydland and Prescott (1977) and Barro and Gordon (1983).

empirically. One of the most prominent commitment devices considered in the modern debate about monetary policy is reputation. The argument is that if a monetary authority restrains from debasing for a long period, then it will earn a reputation as trustworthy. Then the gain to this monetary authority from debasing is offset by the fact that in the future both parties will be in the bad equilibrium. This may be sufficient to sustain a "reputational" equilibrium.[23]

One result that is general to reputational equilibria is their sensitivity to the interest rate, or rate at which the authorities discount the future. The intuition is clear – if the benefit of revenue today is far more important than the possibility of perpetual gains in the future, then debasement will pay. This result may be useful in understanding the relative stability of currencies for long periods of time, followed by periods of debasement, often associated with war times. However, while intuitively compelling, the theoretical underpinnings of reputational equilibria are weak. Explicit results depend on deriving the optimal "punishment" for a monetary authority that "cheats" and results are very assumption sensitive.

CONCLUSIONS

The monetary system of a market economy needs to provide a medium of exchange for a variety of scales of

---

[23] See, for example, Bordo and Kydland (1995) and Bordo and Rockoff (1996).

transaction. This chapter has shown how attempts to provide a range of denominations could amplify the problems of counterfeiting, debasement and undervaluation. The two following chapters look at the empirical evidence on the severity of these problems for larger and smaller denominations, respectively. For larger denominations, the usual solution was to adopt a bimetallic standard using both gold and silver coins. This avoided the problems of low-fineness coins but made undervaluation a chronic concern.[24] For smaller denominations, the solutions were more heterogeneous across countries and centuries: copper (both full-bodied and token coins) and low-fineness silver coins were frequently used, making counterfeiting as much of a concern as undervaluation.

---

[24] The growing use of bank notes in England in the eighteenth century presented an additional solution to the large-denomination problem.

3

Bimetallism before the
Nineteenth Century

The stability of the price of gold under the classical gold standard has encouraged the idea that a commodity money standard anchors the price level. Yet, looking at the history of commodity money standards in England and France from the midfourteenth century to the early nineteenth century, we see that the value of an ounce of silver (or gold) showed a systematic upward trend interspersed with a few relatively brief periods of extremely rapid depreciation (Figures 3.1 and 3.2). In this chapter I document the extent of that depreciation, "how" it occurred and why.

The general trend has three broad characteristics: greater depreciation in France than in England, greater depreciation of gold than of silver, and more frequent depreciation before the midseventeenth century than after. I argue that these patterns can each be explained by the technology of commodity money, which created "good" and "bad" monies, and the response of the monetary authorities to undervaluation, which was to raise the value of the "good" money, that is, to depreciate it. The greater depreciation in France reflected the use of "billon" coinage, which encouraged undervaluation. The increase in the relative price of gold to silver over the period meant gold was more often undervalued than silver; and, the clipping of coins, which had caused newly minted coins to be undervalued, was eliminated by the shift from hammered coins to milled coinage in the midseventeenth century.

Gross seignorage rates were typically quite low, and fiscal motives were not the major cause of the trend depreciation. However, fiscal motives were not completely absent and were most obvious during the episodes of debasement. Debasements are puzzling phenomena, as

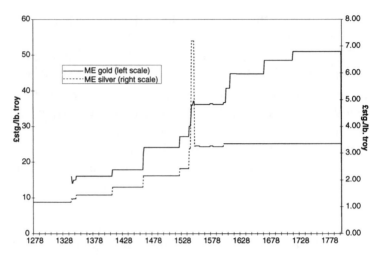

Figure 3.1. Mint equivalent of gold and silver in England,
1360–1789. Source: Challis (1992: appendix 2).

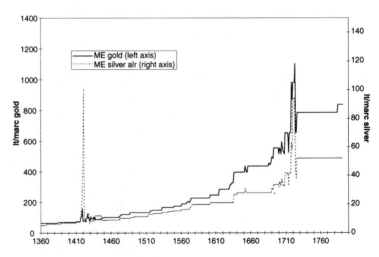

Figure 3.2. Mint equivalents of gold and silver in France,
1360–1789. Source: Appendix.

Rolnick et al. (1996) have pointed out in the context of medieval debasements. Without making much progress on these puzzles, I argue that we should be equally concerned with explaining the lack of debasements, given their extreme profitability, and with explaining modern debasements.

The chapter begins with a brief discussion of the evolution of money standards in England and France from the time of Charlemagne to the midfourteenth century. Then, I describe the construction of a new annual data set on mint equivalents, mint prices and seignorage rates for the two countries from 1360 to 1800.[1] The following section describes the technology of coining in the medieval period and how it changed in the sixteenth and seventeenth centuries. The body of the chapter then examines the path and causes of depreciation over the period, looking first at the long-run trends and then at the debasement episodes.

HISTORICAL BACKGROUND

The monetary experience of France between the Carolingian reforms and the stabilisation of 1360 follows the generic history outlined in Chapter 1. The decline in the central power of the Empire led to a proliferation of feudal mints, which competed against each other. As noted in Chapter 2, at least in the short run, the mints, had a double incentive to debase the coinage. They could raise

---

[1] The choice of starting date is conditioned by the introduction of large silver and gold coins into the monetary system in the mid-fourteenth century.

the seignorage rate and, by raising the mint price, the quantity of silver going to the mint. But there were also constraints on debasement. In some areas citizens contracted with the feudal lord to pay a tax ("monetagium") in return for a commitment not to debase the coinage. In addition, reputation effects eventually muted the gains. For example, by 1200 Bisson (1979: 74) reports of the coinage of Melgueil that, it was "a coinage, still thoroughly seigniorial, that was too popular for its proprietor to risk abusing".

By the end of the twelfth century there were four main coinages in France (Spufford (1986: 164)): the deniers of Provins in the east, Tours in the west, Paris in the north and Melgueil in the south. The reduction in the number of mints in France reflected the preference for a common currency, particularly with the expansion of trade. In addition the king had extended the domain of the royal coinages as the kingdom of France expanded.

Augmentation of the coinage from the single penny/ denier denomination began in the midthirteenth century. The French silver "gros" was introduced in 1266 and became a widely used coin throughout the following century. The first French gold coin (the "*écu*") was minted simultaneously but met with less success. Spufford (1986) states that the first commonly minted gold coin was the franc issued in 1360, after the debasement of the early years of the Hundred Years War. However, Miskimin (1963) records large gold coinages in 1313–17 and again in 1339.

The first century of multiple denominations in France featured depreciation and debasement, reflecting bimetallic problems, competition between mints and fiscal difficulties arising from wars with England and Flanders

(1295–1313). The first part of the Hundred Years War explains much of the debasement of 1337–60, when there were eighty-seven different changes to the coinage. An underlying difficulty was the lack of coordination of the traditional denier coinage with the high-fineness silver and gold coinages. Thus, Mayhew notes that the chronic increase in the value of the gold and silver coins occurred because the value of gold and silver had risen in the market. As in the majority of the literature, he is not specific about the numeraire, but implicitly it is the billon/denier coinage.

Although England was not a part of the Holy Roman Empire, it too had only a penny coinage until the mid-thirteenth century. However, there was considerably less debasement of the penny in England than on the continent: the penny, which contained 1.55 grams of sterling silver in the ninth century, still had 1.4 grams sterling silver in the late thirteenth century.[2] This stability is interesting because it foreshadows the stability of the pound sterling in the modern period and may help explain Britain's unique monetary stability.

The absence of large-scale debasement in the medieval period reflected the insular nature of England and the centralized control over minting throughout much of the land.[3] Mayhew (1988: 26) argues that a considerable part

---

[2] The weight then fell to 1.2 gms. by the mid-fourteenth century, see below. Feaveayear (1963) argues that the decline in the weight over the medieval period was due to "renewals" which simply reflected the wear of the coins.

[3] Prestwich (1982: 52), in discussing the uses of coins in the late thirteenth century, states that "minting was a virtual royal monopoly by that time".

47

of the debasement in continental Europe was motivated by competition between neighbouring mints, each one slightly undercutting its neighbour by issuing deniers with slightly less pure silver, and therefore being able to offer a slightly higher mint price. Such slight debasements were profitable for minter and citizen alike because payments were still made in deniers, or indeed bags of undifferentiated deniers, without regard to the source of the coins. A mint that did not offset its neighbour's debasement would lose customers to the debaser. Centralisation eliminated this incentive.

The first century of gold and large silver coins in England proceeded with the same mixed success as in France. The issue of the gold penny in 1257 met with such lack of enthusiasm that Craig (1963) has no record of any gold issue until the introduction of the gold florin in 1343 (immediately superseded by the "noble" in 1344). The groat met with similar apathy and though first mooted in 1279, was not regularly issued until 1351. There were two noteworthy characteristics of the groat. Firstly, it was about the same size and silver content as the gros, but while the gros was valued at 12 denier tournois (df), the groat was valued at only 4d sterling (stg.), indicating that the French denier had about one-third the silver content of the English penny. Secondly, it contained precisely four times as much silver as the penny and continued to be issued in that proportion. Thus a major source of undervaluation of the large silver and gold coins of France was not present in England. (The cost was a lack of small-denomination coins, which we explore in Chapter 4.)

Bimetallism before the Nineteenth Century

The use of bimetallic standards to supply multiple denomination media of exchange persisted from the thirteenth to the nineteenth century. The remainder of this chapter explores the difficulties posed by such a commodity money standard and in particular the role of undervaluation and fiscal motives in the gradual depreciation of the units of account.

Recall that depreciation is an increase in the unit of account value of a weight of gold or silver, that is, an increase in the mint equivalent of gold or silver. Figures 3.1 and 3.2 show the mint equivalent of gold and silver, in England and France respectively, from the midfourteenth century to the end of the eighteenth century. The compilation of single annual series for each metal in each country required two arbitrary restrictions. Firstly, there was on occasion more than one change in the mint equivalent in any one year, and I have taken the last change in each calendar year. This is not a problem for most years but is a serious problem during debasement episodes, and the data should not be used for detailed analysis of debasement episodes.

The second restriction imposed was the use of only one coin of each metal at any point in time, whereas in fact there were typically multiple coins of both silver and gold, and (with the exception of the English silver coinage) often these coins had different mint equivalents. Again this restriction is not always a problem. It is most severe for the French silver coinage. The fineness and mint equivalents of the competing gold coins rarely differed greatly, but in France the silver coinage, particularly in the late medieval and early modern period, included billon coins of about 50% fineness, whose mint equivalent could vary from that of the finer silver coins. When competing coins were issued, I have chosen the coin from which to calculate the mint equivalent on the basis of: the extent of circulation (I have not used coins for which there is evidence of very limited issues); the fineness of the coin (I have preferred high-fineness coins)[4]; and the period over which the coin was produced (I have preferred coins that were issued for a long period to maintain a consistent series).

The mint equivalent in England is measured in pounds sterling per pound troy, and in France in *livres tournois per marc Parisis*. The mint equivalent is per marc of pure metal.[5] The basic sources of the data are de Wailly (1857) for France, and Challis (1992) for England. For the mint equivalent during the Dauphin's debasement from 1417–21 I use Rolnick et al. (1996). The data underlying the figures are presented in the appendix, which also states whether a depreciation came about because of a debasement (and whether by a change in fineness or change in weight) or an enhancement.

The data have a number of characteristics that stand

---

[4] As shown in Chapter 4, the mint equivalent of the French billon was usually close to that of the high-fineness silver coins.

[5] 1 lb. troy = 373.25 gms. = 1.526 marcs Parisis; therefore, to establish a common base multiply the French mint equivalent by 1.526 to get livre tournois per pound troy. French coin weights and finenesses were often stated in terms of silver argent-le-roi, which is 23/24 fine, so the numbers here will differ from those in documents based on silver argent-le-roi.

out. Perhaps the most obvious are that in both countries the mint equivalent of both gold and silver rose over time, and that that rise reflected a ratcheting effect where there were many step increases in the mint equivalent and few decreases. The extent of depreciation in both countries was greater for gold than for silver, and for both metals was greater in France than in England. If we take 1360 values as 100, then by 1790 the English mint equivalent for silver (for gold) had risen to 233 (317), and the French mint equivalent had risen to 991 (1,328). A further characteristic of the data is that in both countries there were long periods of intermittent small, but permanent, depreciations punctuated by bursts of transitory very large depreciations.

This data set is also used to calculate mint ratios (the ratio of the mint equivalent of gold to silver) for England and France. The general trend is of a fairly stable ratio around 11 from 1360 to 1600 followed by a secular increase to about 15 through the seventeenth century (see Figure 3.3). Around this trend there are many short-term fluctuations. The three debasement periods stand out, in each case by indicating greater debasement of silver than gold coinage. In addition the French mint ratio is more volatile than that of England. The volatility typically reflected a decision to increase the mint equivalent of the gold coin without increasing the mint equivalent of the silver coin. The return to the trend reflected, not a decrease in the mint equivalent of the gold coin, but a proportionate increase in the mint equivalent of the silver coin.

Finally, I use data on mint prices (from the same sources) to compute gross seignorage rates on coins of each metal for the two countries (Figures 3.4 and 3.5).

51

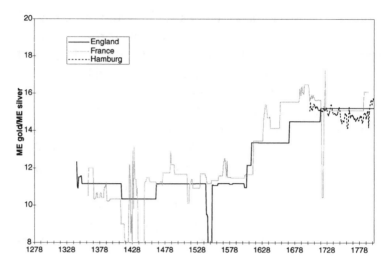

Figure 3.3. Mint ratios in England and France, 1360–1789.
Sources: Figures 3.1, 3.2, and Shaw (1896).

In the absence of a debasement, seignorage rates were relatively low, and typically lower for gold than for silver. In England, the rates were essentially under 5% for both metals. In France, typical seignorage rates were higher, but typically under 10%. Episodes of high seignorage reflected increases in mint equivalent not immediately matched by an increase in the mint price. The short-lived nature of these episodes reflected the fact that the mint price was usually raised very shortly afterwards (see appendix).[6]

---

[6] Negative seignorage rates are somewhat puzzling. During the debasement periods, they reflect a stable mint price while coins are being cried down in value. I interpret this as bad mint price data. More puzzling are the few occasions when seignorage is negative in the absence of debasement.

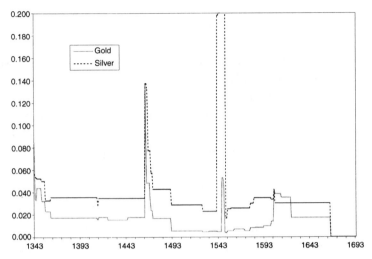

Figure 3.4. Seignorage rates in England, 1360–1789. Source:
Challis (1992: appendix 2).

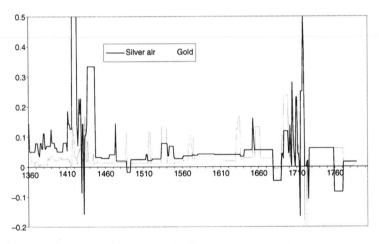

Figure 3.5. Seignorage rates in France, 1360–1789. Source:
Appendix.

53

THE TECHNOLOGY OF COINING

Before turning to separate analyses of the trend towards depreciation in England and France, I will digress slightly to discuss a source of coin undervaluation, and consequently depreciation, that was common to both countries: coin clipping. Clipping involved taking a small piece off the edge of a coin, and profiting by circulating the clipped coin at its official value, while collecting the clippings to melt down and sell as bullion.

The medieval method of coining involved hammering a thin piece of metal (gold or silver) to the desired thickness, then cutting out discs of the appropriate shape, weight and size with scissors. These "blanks" were then placed on an obverse die and struck with a hammer in which the reverse die was embedded (see Illustration 3.1). Apart from the slowness of this process, it produced coins which were heterogeneous in shape and whose impression was frequently not centered on the flan, leaving a part of the coin with no impression. This made the coins vulnerable to clipping.[7]

The circulation of clipped coins at par meant that unclipped coins were relatively undervalued and, as we see below, led to "good" coins circulating at a premium. The elimination of clipping came with the introduction of mechanised minting processes, which made more homogeneous coins. The first application of mechanization to

---

[7] In addition the hammered flans were not smooth enough to receive good impressions, and so it was frequently necessary to use many hammer blows to stamp the impression, which consequently was frequently blurred (Hocking, 1909).

Illustration 3.1. Hammered coinage. Woodcut by Leonhard Beck, 1514–16. Illustration for *Der Weisskunig*, by Maximillian I. Courtesy of Staatsgalerie Stuttgart.

coining is usually attributed to Benvenuto Cellini, who introduced machinery developed by Lazari Bramante and Leonardo da Vinci to the Italian mints in the early sixteenth century (Usher, 1957). The machinery included rolling mills to replace the hammering out of flans, cutting presses to replace the use of shears to make the blanks and

55

Illustration 3.2. Milled coinage. Woodcut from Diderot's *Encyclopedie ou Dictionnaire Raisonée des Sciences*, Paris, 1751, Plate XV. Figures Volume VIII. Courtesy of Special Collections and University Archives Division University of British Columbia.

a screw press for stamping the coins. The rolling presses were powered by horses or water, while the screw press was powered by men (see Illustration 3.2).

The new machinery was used in the Augsberg mint, and in the 1550s Henry II of France, hearing of the equipment from his ambassador there, imported a set of equipment for the Paris mint. However, before the equipment was brought on line, Henry died (1559) and Francis I was unable to overcome the "fierce and bitter" opposition of the moneyers (Hocking, 1909: 72). In 1563 the Cours des monnaies banned the use of machinery for gold and silver coinage, although it continued to be used for copper coinage and medals.

In 1561 an engineer from the Paris mint, Eloi Mestrell, took his knowledge of coining machines to London and attempted to sell the technology to the Royal Mint. As in France the innovations met considerable opposition from the moneyers, and in 1572 the Royal Mint determined that the machinery was inferiour to the use of the hammer. (Mestrell was subsequently hanged for counterfeiting!)

In the early seventeenth century, the mechanised mint in Paris (now located at the Hôtel de Nesle) continued to produce copper coins and to interest the engineers there. Nicholas Briot in the 1620s attempted to reintroduce gold and silver to that mint, but the moneyers' opposition was apparently sufficiently strong that he also left for England, where he met with slightly more success.[8] In 1639, the new director of the Paris mint, Jean Varin, finally convinced the king that the hammered coinage must be replaced, and in 1640 new gold coins called *louis* were introduced (with silver louis the following year) to be made with the screw press. In 1645 all hammered coinage was prohibited.

Briot was hired by the mint in England, and in the 1640s established the modern coining apparatus at the Edinburgh Mint. Royal Mint officials remained opposed to the mechanisation of the mint and were successful in deflecting innovation until the success of the French recoinage and the admitted inadequacy of the English coins made change unavoidable. In 1649 an engineer from the Paris mint, Peter Blondeau, was invited to England to

---

[8] Blanchet and Dieudonné (1916: 195) state that he fled France to avoid his creditors.

introduce the coining machines – rolling mills, cutting presses and screw press – and to develop his own edge-marking tools.[9]

In November 1657, after years of trials, Parliament authorized the funds to purchase machinery for coin production; however, with the restoration of the monarchy in 1660 Blondeau returned to France, and coinage by hammer resumed. On the grounds that it might fall into the wrong hands and be used for counterfeiting, the mint machinery that had been imported was sent to the Edinburgh mint (Challis, 1992: 339). However, King Charles quickly recalled Blondeau, and in 1662 the plans for mechanisation started again, and the mechanised mint finally began operation in 1663. After 1663 all the gold and silver coins were struck by the presses.

Why did it take 150 years for the mechanical coining methods to be adopted in Paris and London? Historians of both mints have blamed the moneyers for the delay in the diffusion of the technology. Le Blanc argues that it was the opposition and rejection of the Cour des monnaies that led to Briot's departure from the Paris mint:

[9] Edge marking involved either printing on the edge of the coin or putting vertical lines across the edge. In the 1550s this was done by the use of a segmented collar around the flan, but this method could only be used for relatively thick coins. As noted in Chapter 4, the English coinage had many very thin coins. Blondeau stated that he had a new technology that could mark thin coins (Hocking, 1909). Coins made by the machinery were originally called "milled" coinage because of the use of a water wheel (mill) to drive the rolling mills. Subsequently, the term "milled coins" has been used to refer to coins with grained edges.

> Tout ce que la cabale et la malice peuvent inven-
> ter fut mis en usage pour faire echouer les dessins
> de Nicholas Briot.... Le chagrin qu'il eut de
> trouver si peu de protection en France l'obligea de
> passer en Angleterre. (cited in Craig, 1953: 147)

Similarly, Roberts-Austen (1884: 810) blamed the self-
interest of the London mint moneyers for their refusal to
adopt mechanisation in the midsixteenth century:

> Prejudice or interest of craftsmen called moneyers
> delayed its [the hammered coinage] entire aban-
> donment in this country until the year 1662
> although ... better methods were well known
> more than a century earlier.

Craig (1953: 152) notes that in 1651 when the
Commonwealth Government asked Blondeau to try out
his machines at the mint "the wrath of the Moneyers
exceeded all bounds".

One plausible explanation for the moneyers' opposition
is that although the coinage would become cost effective
after a certain scale and amount of learning by doing,
at the initial rates it was slower or more costly than
hammering. Alternatively, it may have been that the benefits of the new coinage did not accrue to the people
who bore the costs, and that the moneyers used their priv-
ileged position to prevent an institutional change that
would reduce their number and income. Unfortunately the
data are too fragmentary to make a clear choice between
these hypotheses. Challis (1992: 348) estimates that the
costs of coinage nearly doubled with the mechanical

(i)

(ii)

Illustration 3.3. (i) Hammered crown of Elizabeth I. Courtesy of British Museum. (ii) Milled crown of George I. University of British Columbia.

methods.[10] However, Craig notes that the Company of Moneyers fell from fifty-nine Fellows in 1653 to ten in 1670.

The advantage of the mechanisation was the higher quality of coins (see Illustration 3.3). In both England and

[10] He compared the costs per pound between 1630–34 and 1663–66 when the volume and composition of the coinage were roughly the same, and found that costs in the earlier period were about 4d/£1 and in the latter period were 7.4d/£1.

France, as noted below, the clipping of coins was virtually halted by the introduction of milled (i.e., machine-made) coins. The consequence of this for the monetary system was the reduction in the need for recoinage and the reduction in the problem of undervaluation that clipping had caused.[11] Counterfeiting and culling, however, remained problems, until the further advances in minting technology in the nineteenth century.

THE TREND OF DEPRECIATION:
ENGLAND, 1360–1789

There were four different ways in which a currency could be depreciated. The most common in England and France was an enhancement, sometimes termed "crying up" the money, where a proclamation raised the unit of account value of certain existing coins without any change to the coins. Alternatively a depreciation could be effected by reducing the specie content of an existing coin – a debasement – whether by reducing the weight or reducing the fineness of the coin. Obviously this would not affect the existing coins but only newly minted coins. Finally, a new coin could be introduced with a higher mint equivalent

---

[11] "La frappe au balancier, importée d'Augsbourg, et l'invention de la virole brisée grace à laquelle la tranche peut être imprimée, mirent fin, au XVIIe siecle seulement, a l'industrie rémunératrice des rogneurs" (Sedillot, 1953: 52). Later (p. 76) Sedillot adds that the uniformity of the coins meant that merchants no longer needed to weigh each coin.

61

than the existing coins. In both England and France all four methods are observed.

Depreciation in England occurred in sufficiently few steps that we can treat each in turn, beginning with the three depreciations before the Great Debasement: 1412, 1464 and 1526. In each case the depreciation of the silver coinage involved a reduction in the weight of the coins (shilling, groat, etc.). The depreciation of the gold coinage came through a reduction in the weight of the coins in 1412, while in 1464–65 a new gold coin was introduced (the "ryal") and in 1526 there was an increase in the value of the existing gold coins, and a new coin was introduced (the "crown").

The rationale for the first two changes appears to have been largely the wear of the coins. Feaveryear (1963: 38) states that the reduction in the weight of the coins in 1412 "like the earlier measures of Edward III [1346] merely brought the Mint standard down to something approaching the weight of the actual coins in circulation". Similarly he argues that the change in 1464–65 which increased the de jure mint equivalent by 20% only increased the de facto mint equivalent by 10% since the coins had already been reduced in weight by about 10%.

In August 1526 the legal tender value of all (domestically and foreign- minted) circulating gold coins was increased by 10%. In November a further increase was mandated, to bring the total to 12.5%. In addition, silver coins were reduced in weight by 12.5% and new crowns of 22 carat gold were introduced.[12] The usual explanation of these changes (made explicit in the proclamation of

---

[12] Previously all the gold coins had been 23c 3.5 gr. (99.5%) fineness.

August 1526) is that English coins were undervalued, causing gold coins to be exported to Europe.[13] Yet, this just makes the increase in the mint equivalent of silver, which reinstated the old gold:silver ratio, very hard to explain.

Craig (1953:104) suggested that the changes of 1526 had the same rationale as those of 1351 and 1412, and that "there is no reason to suppose that they went beyond an effort to equate coin with bullion market levels". He is unclear whether the changes in 1351 and 1412 (and 1465) which were attributed by the kings to the high price of bullion, were in fact due to the wear of the coin. (See his p. 74: "the reduction of 1412 probably brought new coin into line with that in circulation; that of 1465 went further for the sake of Exchequer profit, that of 1526 hardly so far"). The changes in 1526 brought a considerable amount of business to the mint, but the low rate of seignorage barely covered costs of production.

After the Great Debasement there was only one depreciation of the silver coinage and that was the relatively minor change in 1601. That change also had its roots in the erosion of the metal content of the coinage through

---

[13] Challis (1978: 68): "as long as this [raising the value of foreign gold coin] was not done the undervalued specie would be bought up and exported. By the same token, if English gold coin, which was also vulnerable as a result of the same changes [increased mint equivalents in France and the Netherlands], was not also to be carried away it too needed to be enhanced in value". Ruding (1840: 303) states that the proclamation of August 1526 attributed the need to increase gold coin values to the high price of gold in Flanders and France, which "attracted all the coins in the realm". Feaveryear (1963: 48) cites the prices of bills of exchange (a ducat in Venice costing 5s in London) as the reason for the increased valuation of gold coins in London.

clipping and wear. The 3.25% reduction in the weight of the silver coins and accompanying increase in the mint price of silver made it profitable to sell the old silver coins to the mint (the mint price being raised to 3.242/– per ounce, and the old mint equivalent of a full-weight coin was 3.24/–, and the majority of the old coin was sold to the mint.

A variety of factors explain the stability of the silver coinage after 1601. As described earlier, improved technology all but eliminated the clipping of coins, a major cause of the reduction in weight of the silver coins, and therefore the undervaluation of freshly minted relative to older silver coins. A second factor is the decision in 1696 to recall the silver coins and let the money holders and mint bear the cost of the losses due to wear. Finally, in the eighteenth century, the monetary authorities essentially gave up on the silver coinage (as well as on the copper coinage, see Chapter 4).

In England the circulation of clipped coins was illegal for most of the period. The law prescribed that a clipped coin should be taken as bullion (or cut in half and confiscated – half the proceeds for the mint and half for the impounder), but, in fact, most continued to circulate. By the time of the Commonwealth (1649–60), the problem was so severe that one of the first debates of the Parliament concerned the circulation of clipped money, and in May 1649 the clipping of money was declared high treason (Ruding, 1840: 409). In part this must have occurred because worn (but not clipped) coin was permitted to circulate as legal tender and the distinction between clipped and worn coin was rather fine.

The mechanisation of the mint has been described in the

preceding section. The changes had the desired effect, and wherever milled coinages were introduced, commentators spoke of the reduction in clipping:

> Even Women and Children (as well as Men) are capable of the Act of Clipping or Rounding. But this Practice of Clipping has never been Exercis'd upon the Mill'd Money, and I think never can be, because of its Thickness and Edging. ... As to counterfeiting, the Hammer'd money is liable thereunto, because the Tools for Resembling the same, are cheap, and easily made and procured, and the Fabrication thereof may be performed in a little Room, and with less Art; so that Smiths and other Artificers can readily attain thereunto. But the Engines for the Mill'd Money are many and very costly, not easie to be procured. ... [The milled money] shews better the true Colour of the Silver, to distinguish its Genuine from its Counterfeit Pieces. (Lowndes, 1695: 223)

But, although mechanisation commenced in the 1660s, it was not until the eighteenth century that the benefits of the milled coinage pertained. Until the end of the seventeenth century the clipped coinage remained in circulation and the new silver coins and the gold coins were both undervalued. The recoinage of 1696, which finally removed the hammered money from the circulation, has been viewed as one of the "defining moments" of the history of the pound sterling (Feaveryear, 1963: 148).

The decision to recoin the silver was taken early in the 1690s, but the question of whether or not the recoinage should be accompanied by a depreciation as in the past involved a five-year debate. There were essentially two positions. Lowndes, Secretary to the Treasury, argued that the money in circulation was all clipped, and that therefore (in the language here) the de facto mint equivalent was about 25% higher than that de jure mint equivalent. He concluded that no wrong would be done by raising the de jure mint equivalent, for example by raising the value of all the milled (i.e., full-weight) silver coins by 25%.[14] Locke argued, conversely, that such a change would involve a violation of contract and that the silver content of the pound should be inviolate. Although history was not on his side, Locke won the debate.

A recoinage without depreciation meant that someone had to "pay" for the de facto appreciation. In 1666 the mint charges had been removed in England so that the mint price and mint equivalent of silver were both 5/2d per troy ounce of sterling silver. The mint therefore had to pay the cost of coining, but the more significant cost was borne by those who had accepted a shilling for 12d and now had to pay it into the mint, where its intrinsic value was about 9d. The majority of that cost was borne by the Exchequer. In February 1696 the state agreed to take clipped coins at their nominal value until May 1696, a deadline which was first extended until late June and then modified by a provision that the mint would buy clipped silver at 5/4d per troy ounce, and the Exchequer agreed to accept clipped silver for taxes and loans at 5/8d until July 1697 (Feaveryear, 1963: 141).

---

[14] Lowndes (1695: 228) concluded that "the Moneys commonly Currant are Diminished near one Half, to wit, in a Proportion something greater than that of Ten to Twenty two".

Despite the economic and political expense, the great recoinage did not solve the problems of the silver coinage for long. During the period from 1700 to 1800, the silver coinage averaged less than £10,000 per annum, with more than half of that being coined in four years (1701, 1709, 1723 and 1746) when political events caused silver to be sold to the mint.[15]

The lack of silver coin output has been attributed, by both contemporaries and historians, to the workings of Gresham's Law. The mint undervalued silver and therefore silver was driven from the circulation. The scarcity of mint output meant that the silver coins that were in circulation tended to be highly worn (or counterfeit). Lord Liverpool (1805: 206), writing in 1796, stated that only the shillings and sixpences remained in circulation and noted that "their deficiency in weight is at present even greater than before the general Recoinage of the Silver Coins in the reign of William III". In 1774 the government responded to the inadequacy of the silver coins by restricting their legal tender to payments of £25 or less (Craig, 1953: 248). In 1787 the scarcity of silver (and copper) coinage led to the creation of a Select Committee on Coin by the Privy Council empowered to make provision for a small denomination coinage (Craig, 1953: 256), which after a brief hiatus and the Napoleonic interlude, affected the changes described in Chapter 5.

The refusal to "call up" the silver in the eighteenth century is as much a forerunner of the stability of the

---

[15] Challis (1992: 433) identifies the capture of a spanish fleet at Vigo in 1702 and Commodore Anson's capture of booty in 1744–55 as the source of large silver sales to the mint.

pound as the recoinage of 1696. Despite the high price of stability (not having a silver coinage), the government would not abandon the value that Locke's triumph had acquired for the pound.

Concerns about the stability of the coinage had not prevented the monetary authorities from depreciating the gold coinage in the seventeenth century. The adjustments (between 1601 and 1612, in 1670 and in 1718) were all responses to the increasing relative value of gold (a result of the increased supplies of silver from the New World). By 1600 the English mint undervalued gold, very little was sold to the mint, and gold was exported from England. The required remedy was to increase the relative value of gold and the king chose to depreciate the gold coinage. The initial adjustment (1601–11) raised the coin ratio from 1 : 11 to 1 : 13, which exceeded the market ratio. The overvaluation of gold tended to cause an outflow of silver from England.[16] In the 1620s policymakers considered making another bimetallic adjustment, but advisors to the king argued that an enhancement of the silver coinage would cause an inflation that would be detrimental to those (such as the king) who had credits fixed in units of account. In the 1660s the English gold : silver ratio again fell below that on the continent, and the king enhanced the gold coins by 6.7%. Finally, in 1717, Sir Isaac Newton, then Master of the Mint, proposed that the guinea be valued at 21/–, which remained its value until 1931.

[16] Supple (1957) convincingly argued that many of the contemporary comments about the shortage of money, usually attributed to mercantilism, in fact reflected a shortage of silver due to its undervaluation.

THE TREND OF DEPRECIATION:
FRANCE, 1360–1789

As noted in the first section of this chapter the French monetary system underwent major transformations between the days of Charlemagne and the mid-fourteenth century. The strong money and centralised mints of Charlemagne had given way to competing feudal mints, which had debased and depreciated their deniers, before a return to more centralised political power and mint organisation, and the introduction of high-fineness gold and silver coins to complement the now billon denier coinage.

Figure 3.2 shows that the "livre tournois" depreciated to a much greater extent and at many more points in time than the pound sterling, but this trend masks an important stability. As Spufford (1988: 310) has pointed out, 1360 saw the introduction of a strong money policy that persisted with only "ephemeral aberrations" during the continued battles of the Hundred Years War. The introduction of a system of direct taxation was key to the new monetary stability (Sedillot, 1953: 73). The fineness of gold coins was not reduced from 1360 until the Dauphin's debasement in 1417. Then, after the restoration of fine gold coinage in 1435, it was only gradually reduced from 24 carat gold to 23 carat gold in four small steps before 1519, after which the fineness of the gold coins did not change until the shift to 22 carat gold in 1709. Similarly, there were five minor reductions in the weight of the écu between 1435 and 1561 (from 70 per marc to 72.5 per marc), and then no changes in coin weights until 1709. As shown in the appendix, the silver coinage showed similar stability.

The stability of the metal content of individual coins implies that the depreciation of the livre occurred through the increase in the legal value of coins, and/or the introduction of new coins. The appendix shows that it was primarily the former: the majority of the depreciations reflected increases in the value of coins. The method of depreciation can help us understand their cause. These depreciations were not used to generate revenue but had the same basic rationale as the more limited depreciation in England: undervalued coins.

In virtually every case of French depreciation there is evidence that the market price of the French coins exceeded their official value prior to depreciation. Each of the edicts of François I (1515–46) (*Ordonnances*, t.1–7) depreciating the coinage included a complaint that greedy merchants had raised the market price of gold and silver above the normal levels. In 1554 Henry II's monetary advisors complained, "Plusieurs personnes indifféremment prennent et allouent les monnayes d'or et d'argent, tant du coing de France qu'estrangères, à plus haut et excessif prix qu'il n'est pas permis par l'ordonnance du Roi" (cited in Levasseur, 1911: 23). Perhaps the clearest example of this behaviour occurred in the years 1568–77, when the official value of the écu changed ten times as the mint tried to catch up with the market price (Spooner, 1972: 151–63; de Wailly, 1857: 78–81). Similarly in the seventeenth century, enhancements are observed after market value changes (Spooner, 1972: 171–96).

Despite the frequency of enhancements, there is evidence that the French attempted to avoid depreciation and

maintain a stable value for the livre tournois.[17] Depreciations, other than those in reaction to undervaluation, were
quite rare, and there is considerable evidence of resistance
to depreciation. For example, debates leading up to the
reform of the monetary system in 1577 were summarized
by Harsin (1928: 51) as follows: "Ce qui est particulière-
ment remarquable dans toutes ces discussions, c'est la con-
ception intransigeante de tous ces auteurs sur la nécessité
d'avoir une monnaie droite". Throughout the sixteenth
and seventeenth centuries there were frequent instances
when the mint price was not raised along with the mint
equivalent because the king hoped the depreciation was
temporary and planned to return mint equivalents to their
initial levels after a short period of time. Invariably, after
a few years, as it became clear that the coin values would
not fall, the mint price was raised, returning the rate of
seignorage to its "normal" level.

The explanation for the more frequent depreciation in
early modern France than in England reflects the more
widespread use of billon and copper coinage and consequent greater frequency of undervaluation:

> In all those Countries where base money is
> current, there the price of Gold and Silver is daily
> raised by the people, not only without the Ordi-
> nance of the State, but contrary to, and in despight
> of all Prohibitions ... so it is in France; although

[17] The relationship between the increased stability of the unit of
account (and the resulting decrease in the cost of using money for
transactions) and the very large decline in velocity over this period
is interesting but outside the scope of this book (see Riley and
McCusker, 1983).

the Ordinance for the value of the Gold and Silver
may securely be maintained by this help, that no
Forrein Coin is there current; yet when you come
to change base Money for Silver or Gold you shall
find how the people there raise the price unto you
of the purer Money. (Vaughan, 1675: 32)

Other sources of undervaluation were common to
England and France. The hammered coinage was subject
to clipping, which as in England meant that the newly
minted coins would be undervalued compared to the coins
in circulation. As early as 1550, Henry II considered the
mechanisation of the mint as a way of defeating the "bil-
lonneurs", those who took advantage of the heterogeneity
of the coins emitted by the mint and culled the heavier
coins. Yet, as noted above, the experiment was unsuccess-
ful, and hammering and clipping continued until 1639.
Unlike the English mechanisation in the 1660s, the introduction of the mechanisation was accompanied by a
recoinage, which called in the old hammered silver and
gold coins. As in England however, the mechanisation
essentially eliminated the clipping of coins: "the Teston
made in the Mill hath not been seen clipped in France"
(Vaughan, 1675: 55).

The other systematic influence was the dramatic rise in
the relative market price of gold and silver, which affected
the French coinage as much as it had the English. The ratio
of mint equivalents was increased from 11.6 in 1603 to 15.4
in 1632 by successive increases in the value of the *écu au
soleil* from 3.25 livres tournois in 1603 to 4.2 livres tournois
in 1632. The silver coinage was not changed during the

period. The seignorage earned from the coinage had been minimal throughout the seventeenth century, and in 1679, the French followed the English in renouncing coinage charges, including seignorage, although unlike in England the charges were reintroduced.

The later part of the seventeenth and early eighteenth centuries saw considerable monetary instability culminating in the innovations of John Law (see below), but following the recoinage of 1726 there was a period of calm that continued essentially until the revolution. This stability is the more surprising given the fiscal difficulties of the Crown, primarily caused by its military expenditures; in 1763 the Crown was virtually bankrupt. The only change to the coinage was the 6.7% reduction of the weight of the gold louis in 1785. Calonne, Minister of Finance, argued that this change was necessary because gold was undervalued at the mint.[18] The ratio of mint equivalents established in 1726 was 14.45 (785.45/54.33) and the ratio of mint prices was 14.5. The English ratio at the time was 15.2, and the average relative price in the Hamburg market was about 14.7 in the 1770s. Thus, gold was slightly undervalued at the French mint. The change raised the value of gold to 15.5 times that of silver, in excess of both the market rate and the English ratio, which was known to overvalue gold. This provided sustenance for the political foes of Calonne who argued that the change was simply a fiscal manoeuvre to generate seignorage revenue. Indeed, by raising the mint price to 828.6 livres tournois per marc, the mint was able to maintain a seignorage rate of 1.1% and

---

[18] Thuillier (1983: 11–34) describes Calonne's reform.

to attract old louis to the mint (with the usual caveat that
if they traded at the market premium of 5.5% they would
remain in circulation).

HENRY VIII'S DEBASEMENT, 1542–60

The Great Debasement is notable because a dramatic
decrease in the silver and gold content of the pound sterling created vast profits for the Crown. The combination
of high seignorage rates and very large volumes of coinage
created very high revenues for the Crown. Given that the
majority of this revenue was earned through taxes on sales
of gold and silver to the mint, the two puzzles are why so
much gold and silver was sold to the mint and, given the
profit rates, why debasement was so rare. The former question I will try to answer by describing the process of
debasement in some detail; the latter is left for the end of
the chapter.

A sketch of the chronology and characteristics of the
Debasement is set out in Table 3.1. The table is compiled
primarily from Challis (1978), but where he does not state
the coinage charges, they are taken from Gould (1970).[19]
The basic information in the table is the value, fineness,
weight of each coin and the coinage charges. That information is then used to calculate the mint equivalent (col.

---

[19] The two sources contain a few inconsistencies, most of which are not
central to the issues dealt with below. The most significant are their
differing statements about the fineness of the groats mandated in
1542, which Gould states as 10 oz. fine. (Gould also states different
seignorage rates for the silver coinage in 1544.)

Table 3.1. *Henry VIII's Debasement*

		Coin	Face Value (shillings)	Fineness (carats)	Weight (grains)	Coinage Charge (sh/lb)	Mint Equivalent (£stg./lb)	Mint Price (£stg./lb)	Mint Equivalent (pure) (£stg./lb)	Mint Price (pure) (£stg./lb)
		1	2	3	4	5	6	7	8	9
Gold										
6-Apr	1533	sovereign	22.5	23.875	240.00	2.75	27.00	26.86	27.14	27.00
16-May	1542	sovereign	20	23.000	200.00	24.00	28.80	27.60	30.05	28.80
27-Mar	1545*	sovereign	20	22.000	192.00	50.00	30.00	27.50	32.73	30.00
1-Apr	1546*	sovereign	20	20.000	192.00	90.00	30.00	25.50	36.00	30.60
16-Feb	1548*	sovereign	20	20.000	192.00	20.00	30.00	29.00	36.00	34.80
24-Jan	1549*	sovereign	20	22.000	169.41	20.00	34.00	33.00	37.09	36.00
5-Oct	1551	sovereign	30	23.875	240.00	2.75	36.00	35.86	36.19	36.05
20-Aug	1553	sovereign	30	23.875	240.00	4.00	36.00	35.80	36.19	35.99
8-Nov	1560	sovereign	30	23.875	240.00	5.00	36.00	35.75	36.19	35.94

Table 3.1. (cont.)

		Coin	Face Value (shillings)	Fineness (carats)	Weight (grains)	Coinage Charge (sh./lb)	Mint Equivalent (£stg./lb)	Mint Price (£stg./lb)	Mint Equivalent (pure) (£stg./lb)	Mint Price (pure) (£stg./lb)
		1	2	3	4	5	6	7	8	9
Silver			(pence)	(oz)	(grains)	(sh./lb)	(£stg./lb)	(£stg./lb)	(£stg./lb)	(£stg./lb)
6-Apr	1533	groat	4	11.10	42.60	1.00	2.25	2.20	2.44	2.38
16-May	1542	groat	4	9.10	40.00	8.00	2.40	2.00	3.16	2.64
28-May	1544*	groat	4	9.00	40.00	8.71	2.40	1.96	3.20	2.62
27-Mar	1545*	groat	4	6.00	40.00	20.00	2.40	1.40	4.80	2.80
1-Apr	1546*	groat	4	4.00	40.00	29.33	2.40	0.93	7.20	2.80
5-Apr	1547	groat	4	4.00	40.00	28.00	2.40	1.00	7.20	3.00
24-Jan	1549*	groat	4	8.00	20.00	28.00	4.80	3.40	7.20	5.10
12-Apr	1549*	groat	4	6.00	26.67	38.00	3.60	1.70	7.20	3.40
14-Apr	1551*	groat	4	3.00	26.67	42.00	3.60	1.50	14.40	6.00
5-Oct	1551	groat	4	11.05	32.00	1.00	3.00	2.95	3.26	3.20
20-Aug	1553	groat	4	11.00	32.00	1.46	3.00	2.93	3.27	3.19
5-Aug	1557	groat	4	11.00	32.00	1.50	3.00	2.93	3.27	3.19
8-Nov	1560	groat	4	11.10	32.00	1.50	3.00	2.93	3.24	3.16

Sources: Challis (1978); Gould (1970).

* Indenture not found; only the fineness and mint price are stated; mint price and coin weights are based on the assumption that coinage charges and face value are unchanged.

6) and mint price (col. 7) for a pound of alloyed metal, and the mint equivalent (col. 8) and mint price (col. 9) per pound of pure metal. While the table summarizes a considerable volume of information, its format excludes some data, of which the most important is the crying down of the coinage in 1551 and 1560. In 1551, when Edward VI ended the issue of debased coins, he reduced the legal tender of all the base money by 50%. As the table shows, however, this was not sufficient to provide an incentive to recoin the base money. It remained in circulation until 1560 when Elizabeth I cried the base money down by a further 25% which did create the necessary incentive and led to the recoinage of most of the base silver coin still in circulation.

A few further comments on Table 3.1 are necessary. The table indicates that the debasement began in May 1542; however, the indenture of May 1542 was not proclaimed, and until May 1544, both gold and silver coins were issued according to the 1533 specifications.[20] Only then did the debased issues begin. The table describes the silver coinage in terms of the groat, but in 1549 to 1553 the mint indentures did not include groats, but rather shillings and crowns. The table presents pro-rated coin values and weights for groats to facilitate comparability with the earlier (and later) data. Finally, the apparent variation in fineness of the silver coins between 1551 and 1560 is more apparent than real. Challis (1992) argues that the difference primarily reflects whether the assay was "out of the fire" or of the comixture before heating.

---

[20] This is stated in all the standard sources: Feaveryear (1963), Craig (1953), Challis (1978) and Gould (1970).

Bimetallism

Turning to the process of debasement, perhaps the biggest surprise is the success of the gold debasement. In the first twenty years of the sixteenth century annual gold coinage averaged about £50,000. In the five years between 1544 and 1549 it averaged £250,000 per annum. As noted in Chapter 2, the two ways that a debasement could attract metal to the mint were firstly by "fooling" agents into taking money without their realizing the seignorage rate had risen, and secondly by raising the mint price above the mint equivalent of the circulating coins so that old coins were worth more at the mint than in circulation.

Very little of the debasement of the gold coin was accomplished – or indeed tried – by the expedient of hoping that receivers of coin would not notice that the coin fineness had been reduced. But, to a greater extent than for the silver coinage, the mint called up the mint price above the existing mint equivalent. In 1542 (or 1544) the mint price of £28.8 would have attracted the earlier issues whose mint equivalent was £27.14. Similarly mint price increases in 1548 would have attracted the first base coins back to the mint. But, this attraction relies on agents circulating gold coins at their official value not the value of their gold content – despite the high seignorage tax (15% at its maximum) this implied.

The debasement of the silver coinage involved higher levels of both seignorage rates and mint output. The average annual output during the debasement was £380,000 (compared to £15,000 in the early sixteenth century). Seignorage rates were approximately 60% from 1545 to 1551. Relative to gold far more of the debasement was accomplished by reducing the fineness of the silver coin, which reflected an objective of "fooling" people: the weight and value of the groat changed very little prior to 1549, so that agents who only cared about the number of groats received would not object to the seignorage tax. The increases in the mint price were used to attract prior issues to the mint but not as extensively as in the case of gold, and the mint equivalent remained constant from 1546 to 1551, with gradual increases in the mint price.

The most significant point to make about the Great Debasement is that the depreciation generated huge profits for the Crown. Challis (1978: 255) estimates that Henry VIII's mint earned net revenues between 1544 and 1551 of about £1.27 million, which, when compared to ordinary annual revenues of about £200,000 (Dietz, 1923), indicates that debasement could be very profitable.[21]

THE DAUPHIN'S DEBASEMENT

As noted above, following the stabilization of 1360, the livre tournois maintained its value for fifty years, but in the early fifteenth century, the monarchy returned to the use of debasement to finance military needs. The debasement has been documented most recently by Nathan Sussman (1993), and his data are illlustrated in Figures 3.6 and 3.7. The mint equivalent and mint price are shown on a log scale, so that the slope of the lines accurately reflects the rate of depreciation.

---

[21] The real revenues increased less, but it is difficult to say how much less. Brown and Hopkins (1981: 11) show wages rising by about 50% from 1540 to 1560.

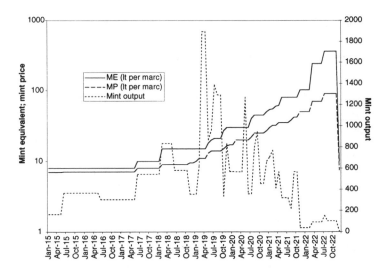

Figure 3.6. Silver mint output during the Dauphin's
debasement, 1415–22. Source: Sussman (1993: 59).

The pattern is similar to the debasement of Henry VIII
and indeed most other debasements. The depreciation of
silver was all accomplished through debasements, and primarily through reductions in the fineness of the coins.
A typical sequence comprised an increase in the mint
price above the old mint equivalent, accompanied by an
increase in the mint equivalent to prevent the seignorage
rate from falling. Then the mint price was gradually raised
without changing the mint equivalent, so that the falling
seignorage rate might attract metal to the mint. Then the
process would begin again.

As Rolnick et al. (1996) have pointed out more gener-
ally, the volumes of coin minted are surprisingly high given
the seignorage rates in excess of 25%. It was only after
November 1421 that mint output fell noticeably below

80

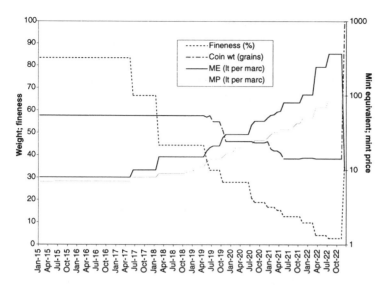

Figure 3.7. Silver mint price and mint equivalent during the Dauphin's debasement, 1415–22. Source: Sussman (1993: 55).

predebasement rates. The consequence of high seignorage rates and large coinage volumes was of course high profit levels. Sussman compares the net revenues from the mint in 1419 and 1420 (about 200,000 marcs of silver) with the typical annual royal revenues in France before the debasement, of 32,000 marcs of silver. The debasement was extremely profitable.

The end of this stage of the debasement coincided with the death of two of the major protagonists (Henry V of England and Charles VI, leader of the Armagnac faction) and the (temporary) return of political stability. The Dauphin, Charles VII, commenced minting 10d blancs that were 37.5% fine and weighed 51 grains, while Henry VI (of England, an infant who by the Treaty of Troyes

inherited the throne of France, except the South) commenced issues of 10d blancs of 42% fineness, and weighing 61 grains. Yet relief was temporary, and until Charles
VII recaptured Paris in 1436 debasement continued to be
used as a source of revenue, and especially as a way of
finding coins to pay the troops.

THE INSTABILITY OF THE
LATE SEVENTEENTH AND
EARLY EIGHTEENTH CENTURIES

The depreciation that occurred intermittently between
1690 and 1726 has generated less debate than the debasements of medieval France. This is surprising, in that the
seventeenth century had been characterized by remarkable stability of the currency despite the domestic troubles
of the Fronde and the international troubles of the Thirty
Years War. Furthermore, the French Crown had far
greater access to substitutes for seignorage revenue by this
time. The debasement ebbed and flowed, but as with the
medieval debasements, fiscal needs determined by military
adventures were the prime movers. The expenses included
the War of the League of Augsburg (1688–97) and the War
of the Spanish Succession (1701–13) and rose to a peak
with the problems resulting from John Law's grandiose
attempts to restore fiscal balance and his subsequent
bankruptcy.

The depreciation differed in an important way from the
medieval debasements. The fineness of both the gold and

silver coins was never lowered, and even changes in the weights of the coins were infrequent (see Tables 3.2 and 3.3). Between 1689 and 1704 there were four overstrikings of the gold and silver coinage. In each case, the existing coins were called down in (legal tender) value and the overstruck coins were then issued at the same value (or only slightly higher) as the previous coins. The profit to the Crown came primarily from the seignorage on the mintings. Despaux (1936: 373) estimated that, at a time when average annual revenues of the Crown were 100 million livres tournois, the recoinages generated 146 million.

Moreover, a second source of profit emerged from the *billets de monnaie*. In 1693 the mint issued the billets as receipts for coins brought to the mint for overstriking, redeemable within a few months. The receipts began to circulate as an alternative for coins and by 1701 the mint was issuing interest-bearing receipts without any coin to back them. By 1706 the number of outstanding billets had dramatically increased and they were accepted only at a discount of 50% (Spooner, 1972: 203).

In 1709 a major recoinage was undertaken. All the old gold and silver coins were demonetized, and a new heavier coinage introduced, but the greater proportional increase in value implied that the currency depreciated by 16%. The currency remained stable until 1713, after which the louis was gradually reduced in value from 20lt to 14lt by September 1715, and the écu followed a similar path from 5lt to 3.5lt.

The death of Louis XIV (1715) and establishment of the regency highlighted the incipient bankruptcy of the monarchy and a second round of depreciation began,

Table 3.2. *Depreciation of the Silver Coinage in 1690–1726*

Year	Coin*	Number per Marc	Initial Value (lt)	Initial ME (lt/marc)	Mint Price (lt/marc)	Depreciation (No. of Stages)	Value When Next Coin Issued (lt)	ME When Next Coin Issued
1690	Écu aux 8 Ls[†]	8.917	3.3	32.1		4 steps down	3.1	30.16
1693	Écu aux palmes[†]	8.917	3.6	35.02	31.3	7 steps down (2 up)	3.5	34.05
1701	Écu aux insigne[†]	8.917	3.8	36.96	32.5	6 steps down	3.4	33.07
1704	Écu de 1704[†]	8.917	4.0	38.91	30.5	10 steps down	3.35	35.29
1709	Écu aux 3 Couronnes	8	4.8	41.89	32.55	(1 up) 12 down	3.5	30.5
1715	Écu de 1715[†]	8	5.0	43.64	34.9	1 up 1 down	6.0	52.36
1718	Écu de Navarre	10	6.0	65.45	43.6	3 down then both	9.0	98.18
1720	Écu de 1720[†]	10	9.0	98.18	65.45	5 steps down	4.0	43.64
1724	Écu de 1724	10.37	4.0	45.27	44.4	3 steps down	3.2	36.22
1726	Écu de 1726	8.33	5.0	45.27	44.4	1 step up	6.0	54.33

* All coins are 11 denier (91.7%) fine.
[†] Coins of the previous issue were overstruck.

Table 3.3. *Depreciation of the Gold Coinage in 1690–1726*

Year	Coin*	Number per Marc	Initial Value	Initial ME (lt/marc)	Mint Price (lt/marc)	Depreciation (No. of Stages)	Value When Next Coin Issued	ME When Next Coin Issued
1690	louis à l'écu†	36.25	12.5	494.32		4 steps down	11.5	454.77
1693	louis of 1693†	36.25	14	553.64	445	5 steps down (2 up)	13.0	514.09
1701	louis of 1701†	36.25	14	553.64	494	6 steps down	12.5	494.32
1704	louis of 1704†	36.25	15	576.81	494	11 steps down	12.5	494.32
1709	louis of 8Ls	30	20	654.54	531	11 steps down	14	458.18
1715	louis of 2 batons†	30	20	654.54	523	1 step down (1 up)	24	785.17
1718	louis à la Croix de Malte	25	36	981.00	523	12 steps down (4 up)	54	1,472.72
1720	louis de 2 Ls†	25	54	1,472.72	1,472	3 steps down	39.6	1,079.99
1723	louis dit mirlitons	37.5	27	1,104.54	1,087	4 steps down	12	490.91
1726	louis de 2 écussons	30	20	654.54	641	(1 up)	24	785.45

* All coins are 22 carat (91.7%) fine.
† Coins of the previous issue were overstruck.
Source: De Wailly (1857).

which culminated in the dramatic depreciation of 1720 that accompanied the final paroxysms of John Law's "system". In late 1715/early 1716 the silver écu and gold louis of 1709 were ordered to be overstruck and reissued at 5lt for the écu and 20lt for the louis, implying a 42% depreciation. In May 1718 the (gold) *louis à la Croix de Malte*, and (silver) *écu de Navarre* were introduced, representing a further 66% depreciation. Further depreciation came as the value of the louis rose from 36lt at its issue to 72lt by July 1720, the *écu de Navarre* similarly rising from 6lt to 12lt by July 1720. But this was the peak of Law's system, and in September they were called in to be overstruck, at 54lt and 9lt respectively.

The final stabilisation of the coinage took six years to effect. In September 1724 the silver *écu aux 8 Ls* was issued at a mint equivalent of 45.27 livres per marc, and the *écu aux lauriers* issued in 1726 maintained the same rate. The gold coinage went through more stages, with a general recoinage in 1723 which replaced the *louis de 2 Ls* with the *louis dit mirlitons* at 27lt, gradually reduced to 23lt. In 1726 another recoinage and issue of a heavier *louis aux lunettes* at an initial rate of 20lt, raised to 24lt in May of that year. As noted above, from May 1726 to 1785 there were no further changes to the coinage.

CONCLUSION

Commodity money standards did not anchor the nominal side of the economy. The history of French and English bimetallic standards shows a secular trend of depreciation punctuated with flare-ups of debasement. Depreciation occurred because under the commodity money standards in place, goods and monies were priced in a unit of account and the monetary authorities chose the value of coins. In large measure monetary authorities – that is, monarchs – did not use this power expediently, and we have seen that the trend depreciation occurred because of technical or physical problems with commodities as a medium of exchange: coins wore out or were clipped; relative market prices of gold and silver changed causing the difficulties that go under the name of Gresham's Law.

Yet there were debasements, and they continue to puzzle economists. Why were they so profitable? And, given those profits, why were they so rare? The profitability of debasement is a puzzle because the profits come from agents voluntarily paying a seignorage tax (Rolnick et al., 1996). The traditional explanation relies heavily on the assumption of circulation by tale. Yet, gold coins, at least, frequently did not circulate by tale but at a market premium, and if coins did circulate by tale, why did they when, at least during debasements, it imposed such high costs on agents?

The model of Velde, Weber and Wright (1996) suggests part of the answer. They show that in a simple random matching search model of money, if some agents are uninformed about the value of a coin (say high or low gold content) then there may be (depending on parameter values) equilibria where the two types of coin circulate concurrently at the same "price". The intuition relies on the fact that (1) since agents only meet potential traders

87

infrequently, there is a cost to not trading and (2) if you take the coin at "par" it is likely that, in turn, you will be able to sell it at "par". The extensive use of changes in fineness of silver coin by the Dauphin and by Henry VIII suggest a clear attempt to "fool" agents, which is consistent with this view. The depreciation in France at the turn of the eighteenth century is harder to explain; in those periods the fineness of the coins was never altered, although mint output levels attained historic highs![22]

The second puzzle raised by debasements concerns their infrequency. In each of the three debasements considered here the fiscal benefits were very large. The costs are harder to identify. Clearly they include both short-run dislocations to the economy as well as the long-run distrust of the monetary authorities that a debasement engendered. Two examples are suggestive. In 1570 Elizabeth I in England considered introducing billon coins to provide a small-denomination coinage (see Chapter 4 for details) but did not do so because her advisors argued that the citizens would believe it was the beginning of another debasement. In 1785 when Calonne adjusted the gold coinage – in a time-honoured response to the undervaluation of gold at the mint – it was widely seen as an attempt by the Crown to exploit its seignorage rights. Similarly, eliminating the ability to manipulate the coinage was a central element of the debate over the reforms to the currency after the French Revolution.

---

[22] This is somewhat exaggerated. There were extensive issues of billon coins from 1693 to 1696, which could be seen as part of the debasement.

Table 3A.1. *England – Silver*

	Mint Price	Mint Equivalent	Coin	Legal Value	Fineness	Weight	Change Legal Value	Change Fineness	Change Weight	Coinage Charges	Seignorage Rate
1343	1.228	1.30	penny	1d	0.925					0.063	0.059
1344	1.213	1.28	penny	1d	0.925	20.30			×	0.058	0.055
1345	1.223	1.29	penny	1d	0.925	20.15			×	0.058	0.055
1346	1.233	1.30	penny	1d	0.925	20.00			×	0.058	0.055
1351	1.373	1.44	penny	1d	0.925	18.00			×	0.058	0.049
1355	1.396	1.44	penny	1d	0.925	18.00				0.038	0.031
1361	1.392	1.44	penny	1d	0.925	18.00				0.042	0.035
1412	1.682	1.73	penny	1d	0.925	15.00			×	0.042	0.029
1413	1.672	1.73	penny	1d	0.925	15.00				0.050	0.034
1464	1.901	2.16	penny	1d	0.925	12.00			×	0.225	0.137
1466	1.910	2.16	penny	1d	0.925	12.00				0.217	0.131
1467	2.007	2.16	penny	1d	0.925	12.00				0.133	0.076
1470	2.045	2.16	penny	1d	0.925	12.00				0.100	0.056
1472	2.074	2.16	penny	1d	0.925	12.00				0.075	0.042
1492	2.102	2.16	penny	1d	0.925	12.00				0.050	0.027

Table 3A.1. (cont.)

	Mint Price	Mint Equivalent	Coin	Legal Value	Fineness	Weight	Change Legal Value	Change Fineness	Change Weight	Coinage Charges	Seignorage Rate
1526	2.376	2.43	penny	1d	0.925	10.65			×	0.050	0.023
1542	2.638	3.17	penny	1d	0.758	10.00		×	×	0.400	0.200
1544	2.620	3.20	penny	1d	0.75	10.00		×		0.435	0.221
1545	2.800	4.80	penny	1d	0.5	10.00		×		1.000	0.714
1546	2.816	7.20	penny	1d	0.333	10.00		×		1.460	1.557
1547	2.996	7.20	penny	1d	0.333	10.00				1.400	1.403
1549	3.400	7.20	shilling	12d	0.5	80.00		×	×	1.900	1.118
1551	3.206	3.26	crown	60d	0.9208	480.00		×	×	0.050	0.017
1553	3.190	3.27	penny	1d	0.9166	8.00		×		0.073	0.025
1557	3.188	3.27	penny	1d	0.9166	8.00				0.075	0.026
1560	3.159	3.24	penny	1d	0.925	8.00		×		0.075	0.026
1578	3.175	3.27	penny	1d	0.9166	8.00		×		0.088	0.030
1582	3.160	3.27	penny	1d	0.9166	8.00				0.101	0.035
1583	3.131	3.24	penny	1d	0.925	8.00		×		0.101	0.035
1601	3.242	3.35	penny	1d	0.925	7.74				0.100	0.033
1604	3.215	3.35	penny	1d	0.925	7.74			×	0.125	0.042
1605	3.242	3.35	penny	1d	0.925	7.74				0.100	0.033
1666	3.350	3.35	penny	1d	0.925	7.74				0.000	0.000

Note: Mint price and equivalent are given in pounds sterling per troy lb pure silver; weight is in troy grains (5760/lb).
Sources: Challis (1992); Feaveryear (1963).

Table 3A.2. *England – Gold*

	Mint Price	Mint Equivalent	Coin	Legal Value	Fineness	Weight	Change Legal Value	Change Fineness	Change Weight	Coinage Charges	Seignorage Rate
1343	14.756	16.00	6 shilling	6/-	1	108.0				1.166	0.084
1344	13.596	14.04	noble	6/8d	1	136.7				0.4166	0.033
1346	14.308	14.93	noble	6/8d	1	128.6			×	0.5833	0.043
1349	14.385	15.01	noble	6/8d	0.9948	128.6		×		0.5833	0.043
1351	15.584	16.08	noble	6/8d	0.9948	120.0			×	0.4625	0.032
1355	15.726	16.08	noble	6/8d	0.9948	120.0				0.33	0.023
1361	15.812	16.08	noble	6/8d	0.9948	120.0				0.25	0.017
1412	17.602	17.87	noble	6/8d	0.9948	108.0			×	0.25	0.015
1413	17.559	17.87	noble	6/8d	0.9948	108.0				0.29	0.018
1423	17.602	17.87	noble	6/8d	0.9948	108.0				0.25	0.015
1445	17.559	17.87	noble	6/8d	0.9948	108.0				0.29	0.018
1464	19.659	22.34	noble	8/4d	0.9948	108.0	×			2.5	0.136
1465	23.015	24.13	ryal	10/-	0.9948	120.0				1.04	0.048
1469	23.353	24.13	ryal	10/-	0.9948	120.0				0.725	0.033
1470	23.567	24.13	ryal	10/-	0.9948	120.0				0.525	0.024
1472	23.728	24.13	ryal	10/-	0.9948	120.0				0.375	0.017
1492	23.996	24.13	ryal	10/-	0.9948	120.0				0.125	0.006
1526	27.014	27.14	sovereign	22/6d	0.9948	240.0				0.125	0.005
1533	27.002	27.14	sovereign	22/6d	0.9948	240.0				0.1375	0.005

Table 3A.2. (cont.)

	Mint Price	Mint Equivalent	Coin	Legal Value	Fineness	Weight	Change Legal Value	Change Fineness	Change Weight	Coinage Charges	Seignorage Rate
1542	29.907	30.05	sovereign	20/-	0.9583	200.0		×	×	0.1375	0.005
1545	32.580	32.73	sovereign	20/-	0.9166	200.0		×		0.1375	0.005
1546	35.835	36.00	sovereign	20/-	0.8333	200.0		×		0.1375	0.005
1547	34.200	36.00	sovereign	20/-	0.8333	200.0				1.5	0.053
1549	35.464	37.10	sovereign	20/-	0.9166	200.0		×		1.5	0.046
1550	36.962	37.10	sovereign	24/-	0.9948	240.0				0.1375	0.004
1551	36.052	36.19	sovereign	30/-	0.9948	240.0	×			0.1375	0.004
1553	35.989	36.19	sovereign	30/-	0.9948	240.0				0.2	0.006
1560	35.939	36.19	sovereign	30/-	0.9948	240.0				0.25	0.007
1572	35.989	36.19	angel	10/-	0.9948	80.0				0.2	0.006
1578	35.984	36.28	angel	10/-	0.9922	80.0		×		0.29375	0.008
1583	35.888	36.19	angel	10/-	0.9948	80.0		×		0.3	0.008
1593	35.618	36.00	sovereign	20/-	0.9166	174.5				0.35	0.011
1601	35.995	36.54	sovereign	20/-	0.9166	171.9			×	0.5	0.015
1604	38.944	40.58	unite	20/-	0.9166	154.8				1.5	0.042
1611	38.125	40.58	unite	20/-	0.9166	154.8			×	2.25	0.064
1612	44.271	44.62	unite	22/-	0.9166	154.9	×			0.32	0.008
1623	43.912	44.73	unite	20/-	0.9166	140.5	×		×	0.75	0.019
1666	44.730	44.73	unite	20/-	0.9166	140.5				0	0.000
1670	48.540	48.54	unite	20/-	0.9166	129.4			×	0	0.000
1717	50.970	50.97	guinea	21/-	0.9166	129.4	×			0	0.000

Note: Mint price and equivalent are given in pounds sterling per troy lb pure gold; weight is in troy grains (5760/lb).
Sources: Challis (1992); Feaveryear (1963).

92

Table 3A.3. *France – Silver*

	Mint Price	Mint Equivalent	Coin	Legal Value	Fineness	Coins per Marc	Change Legal Value	Change Fineness	Change Weight	Coinage Charges	Seignorage Rate
1360	5.3	6.0	denier	1d	0.146	210.00				0.8	0.143
1361	5.0	5.3	gros	15d	1.000	84.00				0.3	0.050
1369	5.8	6.2	gros	15d	0.968	96.00		×	×	0.5	0.078
1372	5.8	6.2	gros	15d	0.976			×		0.4	0.060
1373	5.8	6.0	gros	15d	1.000			×		0.3	0.043
1374	5.8	6.0								0.2	0.034
1375	5.7	6.2	gros	15d	0.976			×		0.5	0.079
1377	5.8	6.2								0.4	0.060
1379	5.4	6.0	gros	15d	1.000			×		0.6	0.111
1381	5.8	6.2	gros	15d	0.976			×		0.4	0.060
1383	5.8	6.2								0.4	0.070
1389	6.0	6.8	blanc	10d	0.458	74.25				0.8	0.125
1390	6.3	6.8								0.5	0.080
1394	6.4	6.8								0.4	0.063
1379	6.4	6.8								0.3	0.051
1405	6.3	6.8								0.5	0.080
1410	6.4	6.8								0.4	0.055
1411	6.8	8.0	blanc	10d	0.417	80.00		×	×	1.3	0.185
1412	7.0	8.0								1.0	0.143
1417	8.0	15.0								7.0	0.875

Table 3A.3. (cont.)

	Mint Price	Mint Equivalent	Coin	Legal Value	Fineness	Coins per Marc	Change Legal Value	Change Fineness	Change Weight	Coinage Charges	Seigniorage Rate
1418	9.5	15.0								5.5	0.579
1419	17.0	30.0								13.0	0.765
1420	27.0	54.0								27.0	1.000
1421	50.0	100.0								50.0	1.000
1422	7.8	10.0	blanc Ch. VII	10d	0.375	90.00	new coin			2.2	0.282
1423	7.0	8.0	blanc Ch. VII	10d	0.417	80.00		×	×	1.0	0.143
1424	7.0	7.5	blanc Ch. VII	10d	0.500	90.00		×	×	0.5	0.071
1425	7.0	8.0	blanc Ch. VII	10d	0.417	80.00		×	×	1.0	0.143
1426	11.0	13.5	blanc Ch. VII	10d	0.250	81.00		×	×	2.5	0.227
1427	8.5	10.0	blanc Ch. VII	10d	0.330	80.00		×	×	1.5	0.176
1428	11.0	13.5	blanc Ch. VII	10d	0.250	81.00		×	×	2.5	0.227
1429	7.0	6.4	blanc Ch. VII	8d	0.417	80.00	×	×	×	-0.6	-0.086
1430	7.0	8.0	blanc Ch. VII	10d	0.417	80.00	×	×	×	1.0	0.143
1432	9.5	8.0								-1.5	-0.158
1433	7.3	8.0								0.8	0.103
1435	9.0	10.0	blanc Ch. VII	10d	0.333	80.00		×		1.0	0.111
1436	7.4	8.0	blanc Ch. VII	10d	0.417	80.00		×		0.6	0.081
1437	9.0	12.0	blanc Ch. VII	10d	0.278	80.00		×		3.0	0.333

Year	Weight (a)	Weight (b)	Name	Nominal	Fineness	Value	Event	Mark 1	Mark 2
1440	7.0	12.0	gros	30d	0.968	68.00	new coin		
1447	8.5	8.8	gros	30d	0.958	69.00			
1455	8.8	9.0	gros	30d	0.958	69.83		×	
1465	8.8	9.1	gros	33d	0.958	69.83		×	×
1473	8.8	10.0	gros	34d	0.958	69.00	×		
1474	10.0	10.2	gros	36d	0.958	69.00	×	×	
1488	11.0	10.8	gros	36d	0.958	72.00	×		
1493	11.0	11.3	teston	10s	0.979	25.50		×	
1513	12.5	13.0	teston	10s	0.937	25.50	new coin		
1515	12.8	13.0	teston	10.5s	0.937	25.50			
1521	13.3	13.6	teston	10.667s	0.937	25.50			
1533	13.3	14.3	teston	11s	0.937	25.50	×		
1541	14.0	14.5	teston	11.33s	0.937	25.50	×		
1543	14.0	15.0	teston	12s	0.937	25.50	×	×	
1549	14.5	15.0	teston	13s	0.937	25.50			
1550	15.0	15.4	teston				×		
1561	15.8	16.3	teston				×		
1573	17.0	17.7	teston				×		
1575	19.0	19.7	franc	1.00L	0.870	17.25	new coin		
1580	19.0	19.8	quart d'écu	0.75L	0.957	25.20	new coin		
1602	20.3	21.1	franc	1.07L	0.870	17.25	×		
1636	25.9	26.8	francs	1.35L	0.870	17.25	×		
1641	26.5	28.0	louis	3.00L	0.957	8.92	new coin		
1652	26.5	30.8	louis	3.39L	0.957	8.92	×		

	Value
5.0	0.714
0.3	0.032
0.3	0.029
0.4	0.041
1.3	0.145
0.2	0.020
-0.2	-0.018
0.3	0.025
0.5	0.042
0.3	0.021
0.4	0.026
1.0	0.078
0.5	0.036
1.0	0.069
0.5	0.032
0.4	0.027
0.6	0.036
0.7	0.040
0.7	0.038
0.8	0.040
0.8	0.040
0.9	0.034
1.5	0.055
4.3	0.161

Table 3A.3. (cont.)

	Mint Price	Mint Equivalent	Coin	Legal Value	Fineness	Coins per Marc	Change Legal Value	Change Fineness	Change Weight	Coinage Charges	Seignorage Rate
1653	26.5	29.4	louis	3.15L	0.957	8.92	×			2.9	0.108
1654	26.5	28.0	louis	3.00L	0.957	8.92	×			1.5	0.055
1679	29.4	28.0	louis							-1.4	-0.047
1690	29.5	30.8	écu aux 8L	3.30L	0.957	8.92	×			1.3	0.043
1692	29.5	30.3	écu 1690	3.25L	0.957	8.92	×			0.8	0.027
1693	30.0	33.6	écu au Palme	3.60L	0.957	8.92	×			3.6	0.119
1699	32.1	33.6								1.5	0.045
1700	30.2	31.7	écu au Palme	3.40L	0.957	8.92	×			1.5	0.050
1701	31.1	35.4	écu de Navarre	3.80L	0.957	8.92	×			4.3	0.137
1702	33.5	34.5	écu de Navarre	3.70L	0.957	8.92	×			1.0	0.028
1703	32.6	32.6	écu de Navarre	3.50L	0.957	8.92	×			0.1	0.002
1704	29.1	37.3	new écu	4.00L	0.957	8.92	×			8.2	0.280
1705	31.7	35.9	écu 1704	3.85L	0.957	8.92	×			4.2	0.133
1706	31.7	33.6	écu 1704	3.60L	0.957	8.92	×			1.9	0.060
1707	32.6	33.1	écu 1704	3.55L	0.957	8.92	×			0.5	0.016
1708	32.6	32.6	écu 1704	3.50L	0.957	8.92	×			0.1	0.002
1709	34.0	41.8	écu (3 crns)	5.00L	0.957	8.92	×		×	7.9	0.231
1711	40.1	41.8			0.957	8.00	×			1.8	0.044

Year										
1713	40.1	40.8	écu 1709	4.87L	0.957	8.00	×		0.7	0.018
1714	40.1	33.5	écu 1709	4.00L	0.957	8.00	×		-6.6	-0.165
1715	33.4	41.8	new écu	5.00L	0.957	8.00	×		8.4	0.251
1718	41.8	62.7	new écu	6.00L	0.957	10.00	×	×	20.9	0.500
1719	41.8	58.5	écu 1718	5.60L	0.957	10.00	×		16.7	0.400
1720	94.1	94.1	new écu	9.00L	0.957	10.00	×		0.0	0.000
1723	71.2	72.1	écu 1720	6.90L	0.957	10.00	×	×	1.0	0.014
1724	42.6	43.4	new écu	4.00L	0.957	10.00	×		0.8	0.020
1725	42.6	38.0	écu of 1724	3.50L	0.957	10.38	×	×	-4.6	-0.108
1726	49.0	52.1	new écu	6.00L	0.957	10.38	×		3.0	0.062
1771	51.2	52.1				8.30	×		0.8	0.016

Note: Mint price and mint equivalent are given in livres tournois per marc silver argent-le-roi.
Sources: De Wailly (1857), Mayhew (1988), Rolnick et al. (1996), Sussman (1993).

Table 3A.4. *France – Gold*

	Mint Price	Mint Equivalent	Coin	Legal Value	Fineness	Coins per Marc	Change Legal Value	Change Fineness	Change Weight	Coinage Charges	Seignorage Rate
1360	60.00	63.00	franc	1.00	24.00	63.0				3.0	0.050
1363	61.00	63.00	franc							2.0	0.033
1364	62.00	63.00	franc							1.0	0.016
1368	62.90	63.00	franc							0.1	0.002
1369	62.90	64.00	denier	1.00	24.00	64.0	NC			1.1	0.017
1372	63.50	64.00	denier							0.5	0.008
1373	63.80	64.00	denier							0.2	0.003
1375	63.50	64.00	denier							0.5	0.008
1385	65.50	67.50	écu de couronne	1.13	24.00	60.0	NC			2.0	0.031
1386	66.00	67.50	écu de couronne							1.5	0.023
1388	66.50	69.00	écu de couronne	1.13	24.00	61.3			×	2.5	0.038
1391	67.00	69.00	écu de couronne							2.0	0.030
1393	67.50	69.00	écu de couronne							1.5	0.022
1394	68.25	69.75	écu de couronne	1.13	24.00	62.0			×	1.5	0.022
1401	67.60	69.75	écu de couronne							2.2	0.032
1403	68.00	69.75	écu de couronne							1.8	0.026
1411	70.00	72.00	écu de couronne			64.0			×	2.0	0.029

				1.00	22.00	96.0	NC					
1413	70.75	72.00	écu de couronne								1.3	0.018
1415	72.00	72.00	écu de couronne								0.0	0.000
1417	92.00	104.50	moutons								12.5	0.136
1418	94.00	104.50	moutons								10.5	0.112
1419	144.00	156.00	moutons	1.50	22.00	96.0	X				12.0	0.083
1420	72.00	74.25	écu d'or	1.13	24.00	66.0	X	X		X	2.3	0.031
1421	76.25	78.75	saluts	1.25	24.00	63.0	X			X	2.5	0.033
1423	78.00	78.75	saluts	1.13	24.00	70.0	X			X	0.8	0.010
1424	87.50	91.30	écus d'or	1.25	23.00	70.0	X	X			3.8	0.043
1426	108.00	114.54	écus d'or	1.50	22.00	70.0					6.5	0.061
1427	90.00	95.45	écu de couronne	1.25	22.00	70.0	X				5.5	0.061
1428	97.50	105.00	écu de couronne	1.25	20.00	70.0	X	X			7.5	0.077
1429	77.00	82.80	écu de couronne	1.13	22.00	67.5	X	X		X	5.8	0.075
1430	77.00	78.54	écu de couronne	1.13	22.00	64.0				X	1.5	0.020
1431	102.00	105.00	royaux	1.50	24.00	70.0		X		X	3.0	0.029
1432	88.00	91.10	écu de couronne	1.13	20.00	67.5	X	X		X	3.1	0.035
1433	78.00	91.10	écu de couronne								13.1	0.168
1435	103.00	105.00	écu de couronne	1.50	24.00	70.0	X	X		X	2.0	0.019
1436	86.00	87.50	écu de couronne	1.25	24.00	70.0	X	X			1.5	0.017
1437	92.00	100.00	écu de couronne	1.25	21.00	70.0			X	X	8.0	0.087
1438	86.25	87.50	écu de couronne	1.25	24.00	70.0			X	X	1.3	0.014

Table 3A.4. (cont.)

	Mint Price	Mint Equivalent	Coin	Legal Value	Fineness	Coins per Marc	Change			Coinage Charges	Seignorage Rate
							Legal Value	Fineness	Weight		
1444	87.50	91.30	écu de couronne	1.25	23.00	70.0		×		3.8	0.043
1445	88.15	89.05	écu de couronne	1.25	23.75	70.5		×	×	0.9	0.010
1447	97.20	97.94	écu de couronne	1.38	23.75	70.5	×			0.7	0.008
1448	97.20	99.00	écu de couronne	1.38	23.50	70.5		×		1.8	0.019
1450	99.00	100.60	écu de couronne	1.38	23.13	70.5		×		1.6	0.016
1455	100.00	101.30	écu de couronne	1.38	23.13	71.0				1.3	0.013
1471	100.00	102.74	écu de couronne	1.38	23.13	72.0			×	2.7	0.027
1473	110.00	113.02	écu de couronne	1.51	23.13	72.0	×		×	3.0	0.027
1475	118.00	119.87	écu au soleil	1.65	23.13	70.0	NC			1.9	0.016
1487	118.00	131.67	écu au soleil	1.81	23.13	70.0	×			13.7	0.116
1488	130.15	131.67	écu au soleil							1.5	0.012
1516	130.15	145.30	écu au soleil	2.00	23.13	70.0	×			15.2	0.116
1519	147.00	148.52	écu au soleil	2.00	23.00	71.2		×		1.5	0.010
1533	147.00	167.09	écu au soleil	2.25	23.00	71.2	×		×	20.1	0.137
1540	165.35	167.09	écu au soleil							1.7	0.011

1550	172.00	174.78	henri	2.50	23.00	67.0	NC		2.8	0.016
1561	185.00	189.13	écu au soleil	2.50	23.00	72.5	×	×	4.1	0.022
1568	185.00	196.70	écu au soleil	2.60	23.00	72.5	×		11.7	0.063
1569	185.00	200.48	écu au soleil	2.65	23.00	72.5	×		15.5	0.084
1570	185.00	204.26	écu au soleil	2.70	23.00	72.5	×		19.3	0.104
1572	185.00	196.70	écu au soleil	2.60	23.00	72.5	×		11.7	0.063
1573	200.00	204.26	écu au soleil	2.70	23.00	72.5	×		4.3	0.021
1574	200.00	219.39	écu au soleil	2.90	23.00	72.5	×		19.4	0.097
1575	222.00	226.96	écu au soleil	3.00	23.00	72.5	×		5.0	0.022
1602	240.50	245.87	écu au soleil	3.25	23.00	72.5	×		5.4	0.022
1615	278.30	283.70	écu au soleil	3.75	23.00	72.5	×		5.4	0.019
1630	278.30	302.61	écu au soleil	4.00	23.00	72.5	×		24.3	0.087
1631	278.30	313.96	écu au soleil	4.15	23.00	72.5	×		35.7	0.128
1633	278.30	325.30	écu au soleil	4.30	23.00	72.5	×		47.0	0.169
1636	384.00	393.39	écu au soleil	5.20	23.00	72.5	×		9.4	0.024
1640	384.00	395.45	louis	10.00	22.00	36.3	NC		11.5	0.030
1652	384.00	435.00	louis	11.00	22.00	36.3	×		51.0	0.133
1653	384.00	415.22	louis	10.50	22.00	36.3	×		31.2	0.081
1654	384.00	395.45	louis	10.00	22.00	36.3			11.5	0.030
1656	384.00	435.00	louis	11.00	22.00	36.3	×		51.0	0.133
1662	423.50	435.00					×		11.5	0.027

Table 3A.4. (cont.)

	Mint Price	Mint Equivalent	Coin	Legal Value	Fineness	Coins per Marc	Change Legal Value	Change Fineness	Change Weight	Coinage Charges	Seignorage Rate
1679	437.46	435.00								-2.5	-0.006
1686	457.00	455.00	Louis	11.50	22.00	36.3	×			-2.0	-0.004
1687	447.00	445.00	Louis	11.25	22.00	36.3	×			-2.0	-0.004
1689	447.00	458.00	Louis	11.60	22.00	36.3	×			11.0	0.025
1690	447.00	494.00	Louis	12.50	22.00	36.3	×			47.0	0.105
1692	447.00	484.00	Louis	12.25	22.00	36.3	×			37.0	0.083
1693	447.00	553.00	New Louis	14.00	22.00	36.3	×			106.0	0.237
1699	502.00	553.00								51.0	0.102
1700	499.00	514.00	1693 Louis	13.00	22.00	36.3	×			15.0	0.030
1701	494.00	553.00	1701 Louis	14.00	22.00	36.3	×			59.0	0.119
1702	495.00	544.00	1701 Louis	13.75	22.00	36.3	×			49.0	0.099
1703	514.00	514.00	1701 Louis	13.00	22.00	36.3	×			0.0	0.000
1704	494.00	593.18	New Louis	15.00	22.00	36.3	×			99.2	0.201
1705	494.00	564.00	1704 Louis	14.25	22.00	36.3	×			70.0	0.142
1706	494.00	534.00	1704 Louis	13.50	22.00	36.3	×			40.0	0.081
1707	523.00	524.00	1704 Louis	13.25	22.00	36.3	×			1.0	0.002

102

Year										
1708	514.00	514.00	1704 Louis	13.00	22.00	36.3	×		0.0	0.000
1709	531.00	654.00	New Louis	20.00	22.00	30.0	NC	×	123.0	0.232
1711	612.00	654.00							42.0	0.069
1713	612.00	638.00	1709 Louis	19.50	22.00	30.0	×		26.0	0.042
1714	612.00	524.00	1709 Louis	16.00	22.00	30.0	×		−88.0	−0.144
1715	523.00	654.00	New Louis	20.00	22.00	30.0	NC		131.0	0.250
1718	654.00	981.81	New Louis	36.00	22.00	25.0	NC	×	327.8	0.501
1719	654.00	873.00	1718 Louis	32.00	22.00	25.0	×		219.0	0.335
1720	1,472.00	981.00	1719 Louis	36.00	22.00	25.0	×		−491.0	−0.334
1723	1,087.60	1,104.00	New Louis	27.00	22.00	37.5	NC	×	16.4	0.015
1724	641.00	654.54	1723 Louis	16.00	22.00	37.5	×		13.5	0.021
1726	740.00	785.45	New Louis	24.00	22.00	30.0	NC	×	45.5	0.061
1771	784.00	785.45							1.5	0.002
1785	828.00	837.82		24.00	22.00	32.0	NC	×	9.8	0.012

Note: Mint price and mint equivalent are given in livres tournois per marc gold.
Source: De Wailly (1857), Mayhew (1988), Rolnick et al. (1996), Sussman (1993).

4

The Issue of
Small-Denomination Coins

Take care of the pence, for the pounds will take
care of themselves.[1]

Previous chapters have argued that the problem of issuing
coins of multiple denominations was central to commodity
monetary standards. The problems were partially resolved
through the use of bimetallic standards with gold and
silver coins, although Chapter 3 argued that bimetallic
standards had an innate tendency to generate undervalued
coins, to which the monetary authorities responded by
depreciation. Part of that undervaluation reflected
changes in the market ratio of gold and silver prices, and
part came from the wear of coins and the clipping of coins,
particularly prior to the mechanisation of minting in the
seventeenth century.

But bimetallism alone could not resolve the need for a
medium of exchange to have multiple denominations of
coins, and the problems caused by this need were particularly apparent at the low end of the denomination spectrum. Although the study of gold and silver coinages
has dominated monetary history, the low-denomination
coinages have in many ways a more important story to tell.
They are significant not only because low-denomination
coins were the principal medium of exchange for the
majority of people but because the difficulties of creating

---

[1] This aphorism is attributed to Lowndes (Secretary to the Treasury)
by the Earl of Chesterfield in his *Letters to his Son*, November, 1747
(*Bartlett's Quotations*). Although it has been taken to imply the need
for thrift, Lowndes had been responsible for the recoinage of 1696,
which was necessitated by the problems that the pence had caused
for the pounds.

a low-denomination coinage percolated up to cause problems for the entire monetary system.

As shown in Figure 2.1 the two ways in which low-denomination coins could be provided were through issues of full-bodied coins – those whose legal value approximately equalled their intrinsic value – and token coins. The former group included very small silver coins, billon coins and copper coins. Token coins were typically made of copper. Neither of these solutions was perfect.

The issue of full-bodied coins was subject to both the technical problems and problems of supply described in Chapter 2. Pure silver coins would need to be very small and therefore inconvenient: an American dime weighs about 2.5 grams, while the English farthing weighed 0.29 grams in 1356 and the penny weighed 0.5 grams in 1660 (Table 4.1). In contrast, pure copper coins with an intrinsic value equal to their face value would have to be very large (for example, the "cartwheel" twopenny coins of England in the 1790s, which weighed 56 gms.)[2] Furthermore, trimetallism would exacerbate the undervaluation problems introduced by bimetallism. The billon coins were easy to counterfeit, either for the monetary authority or by private agents, because the fineness of the coins was hard to detect.

The supply problems were more serious for the low-denomination coins than for the larger gold and silver coins. In the language of Chapter 2, if two silver coins had the same mint price and production costs, the mint equivalent of the large coin would be lower than that of the

---

[2] The coins were everywhere castigated as being "too clumsy for ordinary use" (Brooke, 1932: 221), and were only ordered once.

Issue of Small-Denomination Coins

Table 4.1. *English Small-Denomination Coinages*

a. Silver

Year	Smallest Denomination	Weight (grs.)	Weight (grms.)	Mint Equivalent[a] (s stg./troy lb.)
1356	farthing	4.5	0.29	27
1412	farthing	3.75	0.243	32
1464	farthing	3	0.194	40
1526	farthing	2.67	0.173	45
Great Debasement				
1560	penny	8	0.518	60
1583	halfpenny	4	0.259	60
1601	halfpenny	3.87	0.250	62
1660	penny	7.8	0.505	62

b. Copper

Year	Coinage	Weight (Grains)		Weight (Grams)		Mint Equivalent (d/lb. avoir du pois)
		¼d	½d	¼d	½d	
1613	Harrington	6		0.389		291
1618(?)	Harrington	9		0.583		194
1672–79	Royal	79	159	5	10	22
1693	Corbett	73	146	4.7	9.4	24
1694	Herne	83	166	5.4	10.8	21
1717–75	Royal	76	152	4.9	9.9	23
1797	Boulton					16
1799	Boulton	87	194	6.3	12.6	18
1805	Boulton		146		9.4	24

[a] Per pound of alloyed metal.
[b] Boulton's pennies weighed 437 grains (28 gms.) and his twopenny coins weighed 875 grains (57 gms.).

small coin, so it would be driven out of circulation (for example, melted down) before the smaller coin (Sargent and Velde, 1998). The result would be a glut of the low-denomination coin. In the previous chapter we assumed there were no differences in costs of production for gold and silver coins because the costs were small relative to the value of the coins, but in studying low-denomination coins that assumption can no longer be made.

Token coins were also problematic as the gap between their intrinsic value and their legal value as a medium of exchange provided an incentive for replication.[3] If the coins were convertible (into say full-bodied gold or silver coins), then private agents would have an incentive to replicate them and the authority that had guaranteed convertibility would soon be bankrupt. If they were not convertible, then the monetary authority as well as private agents could profit by "over-issuing" them.

The problem of facilitating an equilibrium between supply and demand for small-denomination coins was not resolved before the nineteenth century. The resolution – as noted by Cipolla (1956), Sargent and Velde (1998) and Redish (1990) – was to issue a "sound" token coinage: Token coins that would not be counterfeit and for which the issuer would make a credible commitment of convertibility. Such a coinage required the use of a technology that enabled token coins to be issued without facing widespread counterfeiting. The transition to such a coinage in nineteenth-century England, France and the United States

---

[3] The distinction between token and full-bodied coins is not black and white when costs of production are a significant proportion of the value of the coin.

is pursued in the subsequent chapters. This chapter describes the attempts to provide low-denomination coinages in England and France prior to the nineteenth century, and shows how the difficulties outlined in this introduction plagued these attempts.

THE SUPPLY OF SMALL-DENOMINATION COINS IN ENGLAND

The English were unique in Europe in never issuing billon coins. As suggested earlier, this may reflect the insular nature of the economy and the much lower degree of debasement in England before the fourteenth century. In the seventeenth century copper coins were issued in an attempt to proved a low-denomination coinage, but in the fourteenth through sixteenth centuries the lack of billon meant that there were some very small silver coins, and difficulties in making change and in making small payments.[4] I begin by describing the silver coinage and then describe the attempts to fill the vacuum by issues of copper coin.

There is considerable evidence of a scarcity of small-denomination silver coins in England during the medieval period. Perhaps the clearest indication is the petitions that the Commons presented to the king and Parliament. From 1351 to 1541, the silver coins minted included the farthing

---

[4] In his history of French minting practices Dumas (1868) addresses exactly this trade-off. Why is it that the French used billon and the English did not? Because if you don't make billon, you have no small change, and if you do they are counterfeit, which is very costly.

111

Bimetallism

(1/4d), halfpenny, penny, half-groat (2d) and groat (4d), and the typical complaint concerned the lack of fractions of a penny. Ruding's (1840: I) history of the coinage makes specific notes of such complaints:

> [In 1380 the Commons complained of the] great inconvenience from the want of halfpennies and farthings and requested that 75% of each pound of metal coined should be in those denominations (p. 238).

> [In 1404] the Commons petitioned the King concerning the great mischief amongst the poor people, for want of halfpennies and farthings of silver (p. 250).

> [In 1422] the Commons complained that little or nothing of small coins was struck, but only nobles and groats to the great harm of the people, and the singular advantage of the master of the mint. (pp. 271–2).

> [In 1444 the Commons complained of the] great hurt of the noble realm for default of halfpennies and farthings of silver (p. 275).

The source of this scarcity lay in the decision after 1356 to make the mint equivalent of all silver coins the same and also to equalise the mint prices. However, an individual could not bring 1 pound (weight) of silver to the mint and ask for it all to be coined into a particular denomination. Nor did the mint exchange different denominations of coins other than by buying the coins as bullion at the going mint price.

Issue of Small-Denomination Coins

In 1356, when the mint began coining farthings at the same rate as pennies, the distribution across the extant denominations of groat, penny, halfpenny and farthing was determined by bargaining between the master of the mint and the king (Craig, 1953: 75). The one-sidedness of the bargain is illustrated by the fact that in the first decade the contracts contained no farthings and less than 10% in half-pennies. The continuous complaints of the lack of farthings and halfpence led to the decision in 1402 that one-sixth of the silver coins would be farthings, and a further sixth half-pennies. But this was a temporary measure, and the complaints persisted. In 1446 another temporary measure was adopted, and Parliament ordered that for two years "light" halfpennies and farthings were to be issued (i.e., coins with a mint equivalent of 35/– not 32/– (Challis, 1992: 710). Changes in the administration of the mint meant that first the Comptroller and then the Board were given the authority to choose the proportions of each denomination to be issued, but complaints of scarcity continued (Craig, 1953: 75). In 1523, a mint indenture stated the proportions of silver coins that were to be issued: 50% groats; 20% half-groats; 20% pennies and 10% halfpennies and farthings.

The scarcity of small coins between 1350 and 1540 was exacerbated by the systematic increase in the value of silver. R. C. Allen's (1998) consumer price index for England, which measures the cost of a fixed basket of goods in grams of silver, fell by approximately 40%, from 0.71 to 0.42 between 1350 and 1540, suggesting that, ceteris paribus, over that period the demand for small-denomination coins rose. The opposite is true after the Great Debasement. The influx of American silver lowered

113

the value of silver, and by 1660 the price index had reached 1.48; that is, the basket that cost 0.42 grams of silver in 1540 cost 1.48 grams of silver in 1660.[5] This inflation would have tended to decrease the demand for the smallest silver coins, and indeed English coins were never again as small as the farthings of 1464 to 1560 (see Table 4.1). The complaints of a scarcity of small coins, however, did not abate.[6]

During the Great Debasement and its aftermath (1542–60) permanent changes were made in the silver coinage. The silver content of the penny (and all the other silver coins in proportion) fell from 10.7 grains troy prior to the debasement, to 8 grains. The issue of farthings and halfpennies was halted and while halfpennies were reintroduced in 1583 (until 1670), the silver farthings were never reinstated. New higher denominations of silver coin, the crown (5/–), half-crown (2/6d), shilling (1/–) and half-shilling (6d) were all introduced.

The lack of farthings was widely complained against. The fall in the silver content of the penny meant that a farthing would be uselessly small, but the halfpenny still had more silver (and more purchasing power) than had the pre-Debasement farthing. In 1570 Elizabeth I's monetary advisors drew up a proclamation for the issue of farthings of only 50% silver, but the proclamation was never

[5] The methodology underlying the index is described in Allen (1998). The index should not be taken as a precise measure of changes in the value of silver, but as an indicator of the order of magnitude. From 1660 to 1760 the index was essentially constant.

[6] The continued scarcity undoubtedly partly reflected the increased demand for coin as urbanization increased both in England and throughout Europe.

promulgated. Snelling (1766) suggests that the queen, who had invested so much in eliminating the base money of her father, could not bring herself to issue base money. A more modern interpretation would be that the queen was investing in a reputation for good money. In 1572 the queen authorized the issue of coins of ¾d and ½d, and in 1583 halfpennies were again minted.

The reintroduction of the halfpennies coincided with the end of the strictly fixed rate for the production of small and large coins as the moneyers were given an extra ½d per pound of silver coined, to compensate them for the extra time it took to size pennies and their fractions. In 1601 this was modified to be 1d per pound, if the output contained at least 4% in groats or less, although the 4% was quickly reduced to 1.5% (Craig, 1953: 424). The larger coins were now produced in fixed proportions: 10% each of crowns and half-shillings, and 40% each of shillings and half-crowns.

The cross-subsidization was permanently modified in the mid-eighteenth century when a schedule of differential fees for each coin was introduced.[7] For gold coins the fees ranged from 6/– per troy pound of 5 guinea coins to 11/3d. for quarter-guineas; for silver coins the range was between 1/5 ¾d per pound weight of crowns, to 3/11 ¼d per pound weight of pennies (Craig, 1953: appendix 3).

---

[7] In 1666 mint charges were abolished, and the costs of minting were paid by taxes on wines and spirits (Feaveryear, 1963: 96). However, the incentives of the mint were determined by the way in which they were reimbursed for coining, which was at a fixed rate per troy pound of coin issued, regardless of denomination, with the exception of the bonus for sizing the silver pennies.

Perhaps James I did not have the same fixation on sound money as Elizabeth; perhaps the need for farthings had become more extreme. For whatever reason, in 1613 he granted a monopoly patent to Lord Harrington to issue copper farthing tokens. The monopoly continued with changes of ownership and specifications until the onset of the English Civil War. It exemplified the problems of copper coinages. The patent stated that farthings were to weigh at least 6 grains, so that a maximum of 24/3d would be coined from one pound weight of copper. Harrington was expected to earn 9/– per pound weight net revenue, and to coin 400 pounds weight per week. All profits over £20,000 were to be remitted to the king. The patentees were permitted to sell the tokens at 21/– in tokens for 20/– sterling (in silver or gold), and for one year they were required to buy them back (rechange) at the same rate. The patent was to run for three years.

Gerard Malynes, whom Harrington hired to issue the tokens, reported on the various means used to encourage their circulation. He made coins that were hard to counterfeit; stood ready to rechange them; gave tradesmen three to four months' credit to disperse them, and broke up a combination of chandlers who were refusing to accept the tokens. At least initially these measures had limited success. After six months only £600 had been uttered and the rechange had been heavy.[8] Peck suggests that the tokens initially issued weighed 6 grains and were washed with tin so that they resembled the old silver farthings. Possibly because of their slow acceptance, the tokens

---

[8] Craig (1953: 141) states that Malynes was imprisoned in 1619, "ruined by being paid back his own farthings".

subsequently weighed 9 grains, which would still leave a reasonable profit for the patentee.[9]

The tokens were not legal tender, but there were many complaints of employers buying tokens and using them to pay wages. In 1616–17 the patent was altered so that tokens could only be sold at par (20/– tokens for 20/– stg.) and the patentees had to rechange the tokens at 21/– tokens for 20/– sterling in the City of London (Ruding, 1840: 372).[10] In 1625 with the accession of Charles I the patent (now held by the Dowager Duchess of Richmond and Sir Francis Crane) was renewed for seventeen years. The clause permitting sales of tokens at 21/– tokens for 20/– sterling was reintroduced and the patentees agreed to pay 100 marks (£66) annually to the king.

By the 1630s there were several prosecutions in the Star Chamber of persons found counterfeiting the tokens. These counterfeits would contain 9 grains of copper and were sold for 24–26/– tokens for 20/– sterling. The patentees found it difficult to distinguish counterfeits and

---

[9] Snelling and Peck both argue that there would be profits from the tokens even if they were nine grains each and were sold (as they were by counterfeiters) at 26/– of tokens for 20/– stg. No data are provided to support this claim. If the profits per pound weight were reduced, under the original terms of the patent, the revenue to the patentee would only be delayed while the king's revenue would decrease.

[10] [Chandlers still make and use unlawful tokens and refuse farthing tokens] "because they are not rechanged into stg. money (which was limited to one year only) and because many people have bought them at the rate of 21/– worth nominal for 20/– stg., and paid wages in them. From henceforth no other tokens are to be circulated, the sale of tokens is to be at par, and an office will be opened where they can be exchanged 21/– worth of tokens for 20/– stg." (Proclamation 17 March 1616–17, #1195).

117

refused to rechange anything they were not sure they had
issued. This of course made people loath to accept tokens,
and in 1634 the patentees issued new coins with a double
ring engraved on them, and proceeded to say only double
ringed coins were clearly theirs. A pamphleteer in 1644
wrote:

> Many poore women who got their living with
> selling of fruit Herbs Fish and other commodities,
> had all their stock in farthings, some 6, 8, 10 to 20/–:
> this poor stock did maintaine them and their chil-
> dren, but upon a sudden this was all lost to their
> utter undoing: Tradesmen of a higher degree in
> many places had at that time 10, 20, 40 yea some
> had 60 pounds worth of tokens in their hands, and
> almost all proved clear losse for the tenth part did
> not prove double rings: it was conceived that at
> that time there was no lesse than the value of one
> hundred thousand pounds in Farthings disperst
> throughout the whole Kingdom and that was all
> lost (the copper excepted) and no remedy could be
> had against the farthing makers.[11]

At the same time a proclamation (20 June 1634, #1678)
reminded the public that no-one was required to take farthing tokens, that wages were not to be paid in tokens, and

[11] Ruding (1840: 403) cites a second pamphlet written in response to
this. The second pamphlet was written by "hundreds of retaylers"
who were in favour of the farthing coinage and who argued that
those opposed to the coinage wished to introduce their own private
tokens.

prohibited the sale of more than 21/– in farthings for 20/– and the tender of more than 2d in farthings. Apparently this proclamation had little effect. In 1635 a further measure to reduce counterfeiting was introduced: tokens were to be issued with a brass plug in the centre, and the patentees were required to rechange both these and the all copper tokens. The pamphleteer (who considered the patentees "the very Caterpillers of this Kingdome") noted that this was "a better marke to make another cheat of a hundred thousand pounds more upon the poore Subject, but all for their good, as is pretended".

The patent came to an end with the onset of the Civil War. In September 1642 Parliament asked the Committee for Propositions to consider the business of making, issuing and rechanging tokens (Ruding, 1840: 398). After further complaints (that the Token House would not rechange the farthings), and Committees, a Committee reported in December 1643 that it did not know whether it would do more harm to demonetize the tokens or leave them in circulation (Ruding, 1840: 402). The utterance of the royal tokens appears to have stopped in 1644: "The great quantity of royal tokens uttered by the patentees, the numbers of counterfeits which were also mixed with them and the patentees refusing to rechange them at last put an intire stop to their currency" (Snelling, 1766: 11).

The vacuum created by the cessation of the issue of royal farthing tokens did not immediately lead to a private issue. However the execution of Charles I on 30 January 1648–49, and the consequent demise of the royal pre-rogative over coining, opened the way for private token issues.[12] These continued until 1679 although few were issued after 1672 when a royal issue was begun and private tokens were prohibited. Immediately after the Restoration in 1660, various proposals were made to Charles II for a copper coinage.[13] However, it was not until 1672 that he introduced a copper coinage. In contrast to the first copper coinage, the coinage was to be done by the Royal Mint rather than contracted out. Furthermore, Charles hoped to reduce the counterfeiting (that is, replicating) problem that had plagued the Harrington coins by requiring the new coins to be sold at cost. Purportedly to encourage their immediate adoption, the coins were made legal tender in payments less than 6d.

While the king's proclamation stated that the coins' value was to equal their cost of production, in fact one pound weight of copper was coined into 44 halfpence (or 88 farthings) and the costs of production were only 18.5 pence per pound. Although the coins were about nine times larger than the Harrington farthings, they were largely counterfeited, leading to an Order-in-Council (11 August 1676) to stop the coining of tokens – except on blanks already in stock. No arrangements were made to rechange the coins and their value quickly declined. The

---

[12] Both towns and tradespeople issued (typically convertible) tokens during the Commonwealth. For an extensive discussion see Boyne (1889–91).

[13] Peck (1960: 602) lists five proposals from 1660, including one from Henry Howard, whose father had held the patent in 1642. In 1661 Henry Slingsby (Deputy Master of the Mint) proposed coining farthings "issued at so little increase of price as to make counterfeiting disadvantageous. To avoid danger of a glut the Mint should be always ready to exchange farthings for silver money" (p. 603).

total coinage over the period 1672–79 amounted to approximately £55,000.

In 1684 a coinage of tin farthings began. It is unclear whether the objective was to help the tin industry (hurt by a decline in the price of tin from 1/– per pound in 1676 to 8d per pound in 1682 (Craig, 1953: 178)), or to help the king's revenues (the king owned a considerable portion of the Cornwall tin mines) or to provide a medium of exchange. Again while stating that coins would circulate at their cost of production, in fact there was a profit of 8d per pound weight when the tin was coined at 20d per pound weight. There is no evidence of facilities for the rechange of these tokens. This coinage seems to have been as unsatisfactory as the previous one. The tokens were easily corroded and easy and profitable to counterfeit, so that "public resentment" caused a stop to the coinage in 1692 after approximately £65,930 had been issued.

Another attempt to provide copper coins began in 1693. Andrew Corbett obtained a nine-year patent to coin 120 tons of copper halfpence and farthings per annum. The coins were to be coined at 24d per pound and Corbett was to pay the king £1,000 per annum. While Corbett agreed to exchange the old tin coins for copper halfpence and farthings, it was estimated that his profit would be of the order of 18 percent. After one year the license was rescinded on the grounds that the coins were light and ill-struck (Craig, 1953: 182), and a seven-year patent was issued to Sir Joseph Herne and associates. The new patentees were to coin 100 tons of copper per annum at a rate of 21d per pound. They were to pay the king £200 per annum and were to exchange up to £200 weekly of tin farthings and halfpence. (There was no arrangement for rechanging the copper coins.) The contract also stated that the coins were to be made of rolled (not cast) copper and that they were to be stamped at the mint.

There were many complaints about the operation of the copper coinage between 1693 and 1698 when the patentees were ordered to stop coining.[14] In March 1694 tradesmen from London and Southwark complained that the copper coins were too light and that they "Could not be put off again under 2 or 3/– in the pound loss" (Ruding, 1840, II: 34). In 1696 similar complaints, compounded by complaints that the patentees would not change the tin farthings and were using cast not rolled copper blanks, were investigated by a House of Commons committee. The committee found that the allegations could not be substantiated. However, two years later there were more complaints of an overabundance, which led to the halt of the coinage. Approximately £100,000 had been coined by the patentees.[15]

In 1713 the mint decided that the copper coinage should be resumed (Craig, 1953: 220), and the next four years were spent in experimenting with ways to mill copper and to assay it.[16] By 1717 the mint still had not developed mills

---

[14] The patentees had only coined 460 tons and asked for compensation for their lost rights. The government noted that the patentees had complained in 1696 of losing money on the coinage and refused damages, although the patentees were no longer required to exchange the tin coins. (Ruding, 1840 II: 56).

[15] These coins were so badly struck that it was common in the 1720s to melt down new coins and make 3/4 weight copies of these older coins. (Craig, 1953: 253)

[16] This resulted in the development of the hammer test: Red, hot pure copper can be beaten thin without cracking.

strong enough to roll the copper and "the public demand for more copper coin had become too insistent to permit any further delay in experimenting" (Peck, 1960: 198). The coins were stamped at the mint, and were issued at 23d per pound. The lightness of the coins (the 1695–99 issue had been at 21d/lb.) in part reflected an increase in the price of copper, (from £112/ton in 1693 to £120/ton) and in part a rise in the mint's profit to 4.25d per pound (Peck, 1960: 199). While Corbett and Herne had been expected to spend £12 per ton on distributing the coins, the Treasury did not allocate funds for the mint to issue the coins so that they were only available at the mint in packets of five and ten shillings (Craig, 1953: 221). Craig estimates that £30,289 were issued between 1717 and 1725.

In 1729 the mint resumed the production of copper coins, at the same rate (23d/lb.) despite a fall in the price of copper. Output was relatively constant between 1729 and 1755, when the coinage was halted after the production of £173,000. The high profit made by the mint was (again) an incentive to counterfeiters. Attempts to curb the counterfeiters focused more on the threat of punishment than on removing the monetary incentives. In 1742 counterfeiting was made punishable by two years' imprisonment while informers earned £10. This appears to have had little effect. Snelling (1766: 44) states that in 1753 "near half (or two-thirds) of the current copper money were counterfeits." There also were complaints of workmen's wages being paid wholly in coppers (Peck, 1960: 204).

The legislation against counterfeits only prohibited the manufacture of coins identical to the mint's issues, and in 1751 a curious issue of "evasions" began. These were privately produced tokens stamped so that they were similar to the mint issues but were clearly distinguishable from them. By 1795 evasions – coins that, while superficially similar to the royal coins, had specific differences allowing their makers to evade the law against counterfeiting – were common. They were typically put into circulation by being sold at half price to wholesalers who in turn sold them at 28–30/– per guinea (Peck, 1960: 206).

The mint issue of copper tokens was briefly resumed in 1762 and 1763, and there was a further £46,454 issued between 1770 and 1775, when again the coinage was stopped because it was believed that there was ample supply (Craig, 1953: 251). But the difference between the mint equivalent of the coins (23d/lb.) and the market price of copper (about 12d/lb.) made counterfeiting the coins exceptionally profitable. Craig (1953: 253) states that "the standard wholesale price was 30 halfpence for a shilling in 1750; it had cheapened to 36 in 1770". This despite legislation in 1771 that made counterfeiting a felony rather than merely a misdemeanor (Peck, 1960: 214).[17] In 1787 the mint estimated that only 8% of copper coin had some tolerable resemblance to the king's coin, and recommended that the copper coins be struck at 12d/lb. rather than the 23d/lb. rate (Craig, 1953: 253). The problems of the copper coinage led to the creation of the Privy Council Committee on coin, whose approach we take up in the next chapter.

To sum up the English experience prior to the nineteenth century: the silver coinages were full-bodied, but therefore the coins were very small and very costly to

---

[17] A misdemeanor typically only resulted in civil proceedings.

make. As the relative price of goods fell from 1350 to 1500, silver coins became smaller and more scarce. After the Great Debasement, the rising price of goods eased the problem somewhat but was accompanied by the introduction of copper coins. At first the copper coins were a privately issued token coinage, but these were counterfeited and with the Restoration a "royal" coinage was issued that began as full-bodied but by the eighteenth century had become a token coinage, which was eventually defeated by counterfeiting.

FRENCH BILLON AND COPPER COINAGES

The French experience with small-denomination coinages is both more complex and less well understood than the English experience. The greater complexity comes from the use of billon as well as copper coins, and also the greater complexity in mint organization. Yet, as in England, experimentation created more failures than successes. I begin by discussing the billon coinages and then the copper coinage. The use of billon substituted for the issue of very small, pure silver coinage; thus in 1521 when the English mint issued farthings weighing 0.194 grams, the smallest high-fineness French silver coin was the teston weighing 9.5 grams. The denier, the smallest French coin, weighed 1 gram; however, it contained only 0.07 grams of silver (see Table 4.2).

In the medieval period the operation of the majority of French mints was leased out to entrepreneurs who bought

Table 4.2. *French Silver and Billon Coinage*

Year	Coin	Number per marc	Fineness (%)	Value	Mint Equivalent	Mint Price
1521	teston	25.5	93.75	10s	13.60	13.25
	double	188	11.4	2d	13.74	12.5
	denier	250	7.3	1d	14.27	
1523	liard	236	22	3d	13.41	
1533	teston	25.5	93.75	10s 6d	14.28	13.25
	douzain	92	35.4	1s	13.00	12.5
1541	teston	25.5	93.75	10s 8d	14.51	14
	douzain	91.24	30.5	1s	14.95	12.5
	liard	231	18.75	3d	15.40	
	double	196	10.4	2d	15.70	
	denier	252	6.25	1d	16.80	
1543	teston	25.5	93.75	11s	15.71	14
1548	douzain	92	30.5	1s	13.00	12.5
1549	teston	25.5	93.75	11s	15.71	14.5
1550	teston	25.5	93.75	11s 4d	15.41	15
	douzain	94	30.4	1s	15.46	14.25
	gros	41	33.3	2s 6d	15.40	14.25
1551	douzain	93.5	29.16	1s	16.03	
	denier	306	6.25	1d	20.40	

Sources: Ordonnances (1902: clvi); Spooner (1972: 331); De Wailly (1857).

the right to operate the mint for a fixed period.[18] The leases were auctioned off and stated the amount of gold and silver that would be coined, with the price being the amount the operator would pay the Crown. Since the mint

[18] Before 1645 each mint had a particular lease, but after 1645 the leases were joined and let together as a general lease (Boizard, 110). Thus John Law obtained the lease in 1719.

equivalent and mint price were fixed, the lease price essentially divided up the difference between the two between the Crown and the operator. (In practice the operators sometimes paid a higher price for metal than the legal mint price, in order to get metal to coin.)

The leases typically stated the quantity of gold, silver and billon to be coined and the holder of the lease had to pay the seignorage to the king whether or not the coin was actually produced.[19] De Saulcy (1877) lists the surviving agreements given for all mints between 1285 and 1545, which often state the type of coin to be minted as well as the quantity. The mints were not permitted to melt down French coins (except during a recoinage) and it is unclear whether a seller of silver to the mint could specify the denomination that they wanted coined. De Wailly (1857) notes different buying prices for high- and low-fineness silver before 1550 but never after that date.

When the large high-fineness silver coins began to be issued in the thirteenth century, the small billon coins continued to be issued, and remained a significant part of the monetary system until the midsixteenth century. But from 1550 on the coinage of low-fineness coins came under attack, both when they were full-bodied in the sense that their mint equivalent was very close to that of the pure (90%+) silver coins, and a fortiori when they were issued to earn seignorage.

Spooner provides data on billon coinage from 1493 to 1725, which are summarized in Figure 4.1. From 1493 to 1549, 8.6 million livres tournois of billon were minted and only 3.3 million livres tournois in silver coins. The coins

---

[19] Until 1647 (see Boizard, 1696: 107).

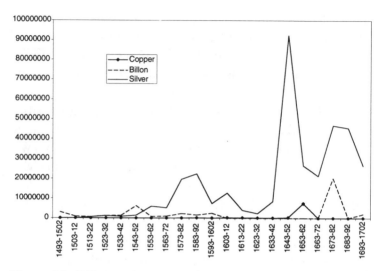

Figure 4.1. Billon and copper coinage in France.

are described in Table 4.2. In addition to the 93% silver
testons, there was the so-called "black" billon – the liards,
deniers and doubles – and "white" billon – the douzains.
Although the black money was less than 10% silver and
the denier weighed only 1 gram (1 marc weight is
244.75 gms.) the coins were valued according to their
specie content: the mint equivalent of the denier was only
5% higher than that of the teston in 1521.

The large quantity of billon in the circulation caused
two problems for the king. Since the billon coins were the
numeraire, if they depreciated relative to the teston,
the value of the teston rose rather than the value of the
billon coins falling. Over the period 1521 to 1550, the king
increased the value of the testons from 10 sols in 1521 to

10.5 in 1533, 10.67 in 1541, 11 in 1543 and 11.3 in 1550 in an attempt to keep up with the market.[20] In addition, the king was the recipient of much of the billon! The king received coin in taxes but frequently had to make overseas payments. In 1540 the minting of testons was forbidden on the grounds (pretext?) that "it was easier to wash or clip than other coins" (*Ordonnances*: xxxv), but two years later, when the king needed coins to pay mercenaries, the minting of testons recommenced.[21]

In 1546, François I again tried to rationalize the coinage, this time by banning the coinage of deniers and doubles, which were "disturbing the circulation of the better coins" (*Ordonnances*: xlvii). In 1550 the new king, Henry II, responded by demonetizing the existing *douzains* and recoined them into lighter finer coins.

Perhaps the most articulate opponent to the billon coinage was Jean Bodin, a leading French economist and early quantity theorist, who recommended the complete elimination of billon coinage in 1568. Bodin was concerned about the ease with which billon coins could be counterfeited, since a piece of 30% fineness was not readily distinguishable from one 25% fine, and since coining methods

---

[20] The precise source of this depreciation is unclear. Historians have noted the general increase in the value of the "good coins" without explaining it specifically; see for example, Blanchet and Dieudonné (1916: 171). Here I attribute it to the deterioration of the billon coins. For example, the douzain, weighing 2.6gms., but having only 35% silver, would have been profitable and easy to counterfeit.

[21] "Ayant besoin de beaucoup d'argent pour la guerre et le transport des deniers du roi, comme douzains et dizains étant très couteux" (*Ordonnances*: xxxv).

at that time relied on the hammer.[22] Foreign counterfeits were a particular problem since – while domestic counterfeiters could be threatened with dire consequences (the records of the mint include bills for the pot in which to boil counterfeiters) counterfeiting foreign coins was not treated as severely – and international co-operation on such matters lay far in the future.[23]

In 1577 in order to stop the incessant increases in the livres tournois value of the coins, Henry III banned the use of livres tournois as a unit of account and ordered that all accounts were to be kept in (gold) écu, with contracts pro-rated at 3 livres tournois, per écu. These reforms provided only temporary relief. Notwithstanding Bodin's comments, the billon coinage was continued but remained problematic. Between 1592 and 1596 2.5 million livres tournois of billon were issued by royal mints (out of a total coinage of 6.6 million livres tournois), during the height of the Wars of Religion. In addition, large numbers of counterfeit 6 sols coins (and copper coins) were reported in the circulation. In September 1602 the value of the (gold) écu was

---

[22] Bodin, (1606: 687). Writing one hundred years later, Rice Vaughan (1675: 31) delivered a similar indictment. "The colour, sound, weight and the other more hidden quantities of the different metals are so confounded as the falsity cannot be discovered but with extream difficulty". Furthermore, he argued (p. 33), "the mixture makes that you cannot extract this penny in pure metal without loss and charge".

[23] Again see Vaughan (1675: 31): "the greatest part of it is not coyned by the State but either counterfeited by Natives or brought in by several Strangers". Testimony to the significance of such counterfeiting is the finds of the tools and raw materials for producing counterfeit French coins in England.

increased by 8%, from 60 to 65 sols tournois (st.), and the silver franc by 6.7%, and the use of livres tournois as a unit of account was resumed.

The heyday of the billon coinage was over, however. In 1603, the billon coinage was halted. No billon coins were minted between 1603 and 1674, when the need to "find a healthy aid to the affairs of the State, and to contribute to the pressing expenses of the war" (ordinance cited in Mayhew, 1988: 135) led to the issue of 2 and 4 sols pieces 10 denier fine in Paris and Lyon. The coins were not only low in fineness but also overvalued by 33% (a mint equivalent of 36lt, compared to 27lt for the silver louis). Overvaluation meant profits for the king but equally made counterfeiting profitable, and the coins were immediately counterfeited. The king responded by limiting their legal tender to not more than 25% of all payments between 10lt and 500lt and in 1679 their value was reduced by 12.5%. The billon coinage was halted, and apart from a small coinage from 1693 to 1700, there was no more billon coined in the seventeenth century.

The eighteenth century saw tighter controls on the billon coinage, which facilitated the stability of the gold and silver coinage.[24] From 1715 to 1739 there was no billon coined, and then a new coinage of sols and double sols with 25% silver content was issued. But this issue was restricted, was not overvalued, and over the entire period 1726 to 1774 billon issues amounted to about 1% of the

---

[24] Stability came only after 1726 when the currency was stabilized after the inflation and depreciation that accompanied John Law's paper money experiments.

Bimetallism

silver coinage with half of that (4 million lt) issued in
1739.[25]

The history of copper coinage in France has a similar
stop-and-go pattern. The first copper coins were deniers
and doubles (2dt) issued in 1578 at the Monnaie du Moulin
using the machinery imported by Henry II twenty years
earlier. They were only legal tender in payments less than
20 sols tournois, but no provision was made for them to be
convertible. The ordinance provided for 20,000 livres to be
minted, and on average 16,000 livres were minted each
year between 1578 and 1585, or about 0.5% of the annual
total coined. Despite these seemingly low quantities, there
were complaints of excessive quantities of copper in circulation even by 1581 (Spooner, 1972: 102), and in 1596
Henry IV stopped the copper coinage for two years.

In an attempt to prevent a glut of copper coinage and a
resulting depreciation of the gold and silver coinage, the
copper coinages were always on government account. In
each case, the contractor was given a specific limit on the
amount that could be coined, and the mints were established at regional centres around the country to avoid a glut
in one region. Mayhew (1988: 128) notes that shipments
of copper between towns, and especially into Paris, were
specifically prohibited. Between 1598 and 1635 copper
coinages continued to be small relative to the value of total
coinage and yet led to continuous complaints of excess, and

[25] The billon coins of the eighteenth century were very close to full-
bodied coins. The sols were 25 percent silver and weighed 1.092 gms.,
making their mint equivalent 44.83lt per marc fine silver. The mint
equivalent of the louis of 1740 (which were 11/12 fine, weighed 29.488
gms. and were valued at 5lt) was 45.27lt/marc. Data computed from
Gadoury and Drouler (1978).

132

of large numbers of counterfeits. The coinage was halted again from 1635 to 1643, but in 1643 a quarter of a million livres tournois in copper coin was issued (according to Blanchet et Dieudonné, 1916: 177, to pay for building the Louvre). Such a large issue, abetted by foreign counterfeits that "flooded in" (Mayhew, 1988: 129), immediately led to an increase in the value of gold and silver coins, and the Cours des monnaies convinced the authorities to suspend the coinage, and halve the value of all the copper coins.

The halt was temporary and in 1654–56, in the aftermath of the civil war known as the Fronde, there was a massive copper recoinage. The stated rationale was to provide low-denomination coins and to drive out foreign copper coins; however, the fiscal advantages were doubtless also significant. The existing coins were to be replaced, and copper *liards* (valued at 3 deniers) were added to the copper coin menu. A total of 7 million livres were coined in three years (compared to 8 million in silver). Spooner (1972: 190) argues that "the copper currency acted like yeast in everyday transactions". Again the Cours des monnaies stepped in, and in July 1658 the liards were reduced in value to 2d, and in November 1664 to 1.5 deniers, and the original doubles were reduced to deniers. In May 1665 the circulation of the doubles was prohibited.[26]

The copper coinage was virtually halted for more than a century.[27] When it resumed in the 1770s it was with a

---

[26] Mayhew (1988: 136) refers to coinages of billon 4 sols pieces (1691) and douzains (1692) and liards in 1693, although Spooner (1972) makes no mention of these coinages and Gadoury and Drouler (1978) do not include them.

[27] Blanchet et Dieudonné mention liard of 1693–1701 and 1713–15; Gadoury and Drouler suggest 100,000lt in 1720–21.

small issue, less than 1 million livres tournois, of sols and demi-sols, which were legal tender only to 6 livres tournois. (Gadoury and Droulers, 1978).

In summary, the billon coins provided a partial solution to the small-denomination problem, yet the ease with which they could be counterfeited and the costs of their production meant that the supply of billon coins was fraught with difficulties. The adoption of copper coins in the sixteenth century represented an attempt to issue small-denomination coins without such problems, yet the same problems of overissue, undervaluation of higher value coins and counterfeiting arose.

CONCLUSION

Simple textbook versions of commodity money standards imply that the quantity of money is determined by such "natural" forces as the stock of gold or silver. But in Chapter 2 it was argued that in practice commodity money standards did not operate so straightforwardly. The need for a variety of denominations precluded the automatic money supply process. In this chapter I have examined how small-denomination coins were supplied in England and France.

Neither country found an efficient, quasi-automatic mechanism to determine the supply of small coins such as the free coinage of gold and silver that determined the quantity of gold and silver coins in circulation. In England the refusal to issue silver coins of less than sterling fineness led to attempts to issue very small pure silver coins –

which generated complaints from producers and consumers alike. Attempts to issue full-bodied copper coins (after 1672) avoided the problems of trimetallism only by the de facto issue of light coins, which promoted counterfeiting, and the issue on government account, which in practice led to minimal issues. In France the billon coinages before the "age-of-copper" caused the problems of scarcity modeled Sargent and Velde (1998) and problems of counterfeiting. After the sixteenth century, copper coinages largely replaced billon, but again the coins were on government account, and in France the fiscal machinations of the monarchy added to the problems of the coinage.

The problems of small-denomination coins were significantly alleviated in the nineteenth century, when the combination of advances in technology and advances in state-building made possible the issue of token coins which were unlikely to be counterfeit, and offers of convertibility of those tokens which were credible. The improvements in the small-denomination coin issues made possible a monometallic standard with the benefit of a range of coin values. We turn now to these developments.

5

Token Coinage and the Gold Standard in the United Kingdom

Token Coinage and the Gold Standard in the U.K.

Previous chapters have argued that a significant part of the currency depreciation in medieval and early modern Europe arose as a response to undervaluation of coins, and that bimetallism caused many of the instances of undervaluation. Bimetallism, however, was mandated by the need for multiple denominations of coins, and technological limits on issuing token monies. The nineteenth century saw widespread abandonment of bimetallic standards for gold standards in Europe, beginning with the United Kingdom. The adoption of the gold standard reflected changes in technology and society which permitted the widespread monetary use of token coins and bank notes. Specifically, improved minting methods reduced the threat of counterfeiting, and the convertibility of bank notes and token coins led to their acceptance.

This chapter examines the adoption of the gold standard in England. The dating of that adoption is somewhat ambiguous since it can be argued that the de facto gold standard began with Sir Isaac Newton's overvaluation of the gold coin in 1717. But here I analyze the de jure adoption of the gold standard in 1816 when by an Act of Parliament (56 Geo. III c.68) the free coinage of silver was suspended, the silver coin was made limited legal tender, and the silver coins were made tokens only. I argue that the introduction of the gold standard was made possible by the implementation of technological innovations in coining, and made successful (after initial hesitancy) by a government commitment to convert the token coins into gold coin.

The historical literature has typically explained the emergence of the gold standard as a matter of happenstance: the legislation of 1816 merely ratified the de facto gold standard that had existed in England since the beginning of the eighteenth century. Feaveryear (1963: 142), for example, argued that "England did not establish the gold standard by any conscious and deliberate act, and it is doubtful whether anyone foresaw that it would establish itself".[1] But such an analysis is too cursory. In the early seventeenth century England had overvalued gold, and silver coin had been driven out of circulation, yet England did not adopt a gold standard. The traditional response to undervaluation in both England and France was to raise the value of coins in the undervalued metal, not to accept a monometallic standard.

Similarly, Frank Fetter and Derek Gregory (1973: 16) concluded that the decision to adopt the gold standard was made "largely on the basis of details of small coin convenience, and not on larger issues of economic policy". But they preface this conclusion with the comment that "It is amazing that a decision of such importance for England, and by England's example for the entire world, should have been made without benefit of full analysis". What I have tried to make clear in the earlier chapters is that it was precisely the "details of small coin convenience" that had necessitated bimetallic standards, for the previous centuries. The only nonsceptical reference that I have seen to the importance of fiduciary money in the evolution of the gold standard is a comment by A. E. Whittlesey, cited in Cipolla (1956: 27): "It is probably not too much to say that this discovery [how to maintain a sound system of fractional money] made possible the rise of the international gold standard".

---

[1] See also Cooper (1987: 44–5) and Kindleberger (1982: 59).

The chapter begins by describing the problems of the silver coinage at the end of the eighteenth century and the remedies proposed by the mint and the government. The changes, whose necessity was recognised by at least 1774, were proposed by Lord Liverpool in 1798, but their implementation was delayed until 1816 by a combination of events including the illness and death of Lord Liverpool and the financial and governmental crises caused by the Napoleonic Wars. After examining the origins of Lord Liverpool's proposals, I examine their implementation, through the construction and equipping of a new Royal Mint and the acceptance by the government of the need to commit to exchange the token silver coins into gold. The final section of the chapter examines the simultaneous changes in the copper coinage. After centuries of uncertainty about how to issue small-denomination coins, the early nineteenth century saw the British government adopt the principles of a "sound" token currency. The raison d'être of bimetallism had been removed and England was on the gold standard.

A PLAN FOR THE SILVER COINAGE

From 1717 to 1774, while annual production of gold coins was in the hundreds of thousands of pounds, there were only six years in which the silver coinage exceeded £10,000. The total silver coinage between 1767 and 1777 was £718. Jenkinson (1805: 208) summarised the state of the circulating silver coins in 1787 and 1798: there were no crowns or half-crowns in circulation, and the shillings and sixpences were all so worn that they had no impression or rough (i.e., milled) edges left by 1787. The shillings were found to be reduced in weight, relative to newly minted weights, by 21% in 1787 and by 25% in 1798; the sixpences by 36% in 1787 and 38% in 1798.

In response to the circulation of underweight gold coins the government had undertaken a major gold recoinage in 1774, with plans to follow this with improvements in the silver coinage. As a temporary measure, they responded to the poor state of the silver coinage by declaring that the silver coins were not legal tender for amounts greater than £25. In 1787 the chaotic state of both the silver and copper coinage led the Privy Council to form a Committee on Coin (henceforth PCC) to determine how to restore the coinage. The Committee began by considering reforms to the copper coinage, but after a year of inquiries did nothing. A decade later, the Committee was reestablished, and although it began again with the copper coinage, it quickly turned to the need for a silver coinage.

The second Committee was chaired by Lord Liverpool, who made a lengthy proposal to the Committee in 1798, in which he reviewed the history of the British currency and recommended the adoption of the gold standard. In the proposal, which he later published in 1805 in the form of a letter to the king, he argued that only gold coins should be full legal tender and that silver and copper coins should be limited legal tender and should be "merely representative coins" (Jenkinson, 1805: 173). He recommended that, unlike gold coins, for which there should be no coining charge, the costs of minting should be charged on the silver and copper coins. He was less clear about the convertibility of the coins and the right of free coinage. He implied that the tokens would be accepted within the country because of their legal tender status. The basic proposal would have allowed the free minting of silver coins. That is, the mint price of silver would be set close to the average market price and the mint equivalent would be the mint price plus coining charges. If, however, the silver coins became undervalued, and therefore exported, the right to sell coins to the mint would be restricted (Jenkinson, 1805: 187).

The origins of Liverpool's ideas are unclear. He had clearly read Adam Smith's *Wealth of Nations*, which had considered the possibility of altering the mint price ratio in order to encourage the concurrent circulation of silver and gold and then gone on to suggest that overvaluing silver and making it limited legal tender might reduce the inconvenience of the bimetallic standard.[2]

Unlike the proposals concerning the return to convertibility of Bank of England notes and the appropriate parity for convertibility, the recommendation to terminate the free coinage of silver prompted little debate either when presented to the PCC or when presented to Parliament as the final report of the PCC. The Committee approved the proposal in principle. In February 1798 Bank of England officials returning from testifying before the Committee reported to directors of the Bank that a coining of silver at a new standard was imminent.[3] Unfortunately the

---

[2] Smith (1776/1978. 147). Smith felt that only bankers would be hurt by the limited legal tender as, during a bank run, they would often stall for time by paying out (and counting out) large sums in sixpences!

[3] MCD: Z G4/27, p. 351, 22/2/1798.

energy of the Committee dissipated with the illness of Lord Liverpool, and the Committee did not meet between 1798 and 1804. There were, however, two changes in the silver coinage in that time. Firstly, when a fall in the relative price of silver led some merchants to attempt to sell silver to the mint, the government responded by "temporarily" suspending the sale of silver to the mint, pending the reformation of the coinage. Meantime, the Bank of England began to issue token silver coins.

When the Committee recommenced its deliberations, monetary reform was precluded by the Restriction Act, which had suspended the convertibility of Bank of England notes and the fact that the government was preoccupied with the needs of the war with France. However, Lord Liverpool had recommended that the mint be modernized and in particular that machinery such as that used by Boulton and Watt at their Soho mint be acquired by the Royal Mint (see Illustration 5.1). The PCC accepted that the new coinage would require new technology, which was perceived to be cheaper, faster (independently important because a silver recoinage would need large output during a short period) and to make the token coinage immune from counterfeiting.

They proceeded to examine how to rebuild the mint. Boulton, who had won the contract for the copper coinage, lobbied hard to sell the Royal Mint his coining apparatus, which had already been bought for use in Russia and Denmark as well as being contracted for many of the private colonial coinages. The apparatus included steam-powered rolling mills and cutting presses (for the blanks) and a steam-powered coining press. Boulton tirelessly advocated its advantages:

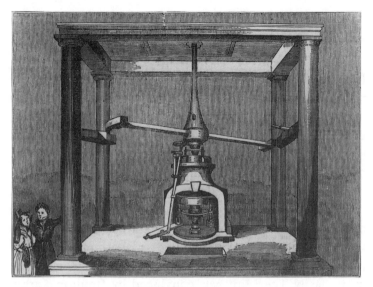

Illustration 5.1. Boulton and Watt's steam-driven coining press. *Saturday Magazine*, April 1836; courtesy of Main Library, University of British Columbia.

The work performed by the Steam Engine will also be perfectly uniform, But that of the Men will vary as their strength respectively does; and even the work of the same Men will not be constantly uniform as there must unavoidably be a difference between the blow of a Man coming fresh to his Work and when fatigued in several hours severe labour: the effect of which will appear in the difference of Diameter and Thickness of the pieces of Coin when examined by a correct steel gauge; whereas if a Steam Engine be used a proper proportion of Power may be measured out for the different sorts of Coin, and when duly adjusted, every

145

blow will be uniformly the same and consequently will produce uniform effects upon the Coins.[4]

Later an independent report commissioned by the Committee supported this claim, stating that if the coining presses were steam-powered, "not only a great saving would be made in manual labour, but the Coin would be much more perfect – advantages which need not be pointed out to Your Lordships".[5]

Boulton argued that the uniformity and excellence of coins made in his mint would make them very hard to counterfeit (see Illustration 5.2). He argued that the coins would not need to have milled edges, that innovation had reduced clipping at the expense of coins whose edges wore more easily. The Mint was convinced by Boulton's arguments and purchased a complete set of mint machinery from Boulton and Watt which was installed between 1805 and 1811.

In 1816, following Napoleon's defeat, the PCC finally submitted its report, which closely resembled the proposals of Lord Liverpool, to Parliament. There was remarkably little debate. The final legislation made the new silver coins legal tender to £2, and mandated the manufacture of 66 pence worth of silver coins per troy ounce of sterling silver. Interestingly, the coins would continue to be made of sterling silver – their weight rather than their fineness would be altered.[6]

---

[4] Board of Trade, "Minutes of the Privy Council Committee on Coin", Vol. 6 (henceforth BT6) 118, p. 108, 9/5/1798.
[5] BT6-118: p. 166, 10/7/1798.
[6] The previous mint equivalent (equal to the mint price) was 62d/oz.

Illustration 5.2. Crown of George IV (produced with Boulton and Watt's press). Courtesy of British Museum.

THE GOLD STANDARD IMPLEMENTED

The old silver coin was to be brought in and exchanged for new at par. In February 1817 the government announced its readiness for the exchange to begin and allowed two weeks for individuals to bring in their old silver coin to exchange it for the new coin. The exchange was fraught with difficulties. The banks, which had promised to assist, avoided the "odium and responsibility"[7] of allowing the exchange to take place on their premises, since it would mean throwing open their buildings to "all Ranks of the Community" and "their Property would be endangered".[8] This attitude stands in contrast to their cooperation with the gold exchange in 1774, doubtless because gold coin was not held by "all ranks of the community".

A second difficulty in implementing the recoinage concerned whether or not to accept the counterfeit coin and

[7] MCT: G8/18, p. 178, 6/2/1817.
[8] M1-54: 6th Head, p. 418, 21/2/1817.

indeed how to distinguish it from the Royal Mint coin. The Master of the Mint suggested that if a teller was uncertain that a coin was good he should call in an intelligent shop-keeper, "such a person probably would be a better judge upon such a subject than a more scientific man".[9] The Master of the Mint (W. W. Pole) also recommended that the tellers be given instructions to give those bringing in coin the benefit of the doubt, with the proviso that "you will be very careful not to divulge the nature of your instructions. Were the full extent of the indulgence to be granted known it is to be feared that many attempts would be made to pass large Counterfeits in the exchange". Nicholas Vansittart, the Chancellor of the Exchequer, commented on these instructions that "it is vain to expect that a secret entrusted to so many will be kept:" and sug-gested that giving express authority to be indulgent was "quite unnecessary and liable to abuse".[10] Lord Liverpool (second Earl and Master of the Mint) agreed with Vansit-tart: "it would be by no means expedient to give as great a latitude as Pole proposes", and the final instructions reflected these views.

If the Coinage Act had been implemented as envisioned by the PCC, the gold standard would have been very short-lived. In 1817 the market price of silver was 5/–, and there-fore the mint price of 5/2d would have induced many people to sell silver to the mint. The limited legal tender of token silver might have somewhat limited the sales, but it is likely that silver coin would have been used whenever possible and would have accumulated in the pockets of retailers, who would be able to dispose of it only at a discount.

[9] M1-54: 6th Head, p. 351.   [10] M1-54: 6th Head, p. 373, 23/9/1816.

At the proclamation of the Coinage Act, however, the clause allowing the public to sell silver to the mint was reserved, since the mint was busy preparing for the exchange, and it was never subsequently promulgated. The mint bought silver at the prevailing market price in the quantity it thought necessary and believed that by limiting the quantity of silver coin supplied it could maintain the value of the coins above the value of their silver content; that is, the supply limitation would give value to the fiat component of the currency. In 1819 the Master of the Mint explained the process in a memo to the Secret Committee of the Lords on Resumption:

> The Mint, having constant communication with the Bank and the London Bankers is enabled to afford information on the state of the silver currency to the Lords of the Treasury; and their Lordships being also in possession of other means of knowing the wants of the country, regulate the issues in such manner as they conceive will best afford the necessary accommodation throughout the Kingdom for the facility of exchange and Commerce without throwing into circulation any superabundance of silver. The silver coinage can never therefore while it is preserved upon its present footing exceed the amount which the Government, from the best information they can procure, conceive to be necessary for the accommodation of the Public.[11]

[11] Mint 1-54: 6th Head, pp. 594–5, 3/5/1819.

By the 1830s the Treasury had realized that the supply limitation was not sufficient to maintain the value of the silver coin and that in fact it was the willingness of the Bank of England to guarantee implicitly the convertibility of the coins at par into gold that gave the silver coin its value. The Bank did this through its willingness to accept silver in unlimited quantities at par. In 1831 Lord Althorp (then Chancellor of the Exchequer) noted that "if the Bank of England refused to receive the silver coin of the Realm in larger sums than that for which it is a legal tender the greatest confusion would be produced in the retail trade of the Metropolis".[12] Indeed the Governor of the Bank of England reported explaining to Lord Althorp, "the necessity of the Bank receiving such coin in order to prevent its being depreciated in the general currency of the Country, to which Lord Althorp assented and admitted the necessity".[13]

The conflict between the Bank's behavior and profit maximisation came to a head in the 1830s. By 1831 the Bank's acceptance of silver coin had yielded an inventory of about £1 million in silver coin.[14] These coins could not be paid out by the Bank in exchange for its notes, and the market value of the silver coins was about 10 percent less than their official value – the difference owing to a decrease in the weight of the coin as a result of wear and tear, and the difference between the mint equivalent of the coins and the market price of silver (still about 5/–). The Bank wished to sell £600,000 of this silver to the mint and,

---

[12] Treasury Papers (henceforth T1) 3141/6277; 3/3/1831.
[13] MCT: G8/26, p. 55, 6/3/1833.
[14] MCD: Eb G4/56, p. 258, 2/1/1834.

perhaps foolishly, suggested that "it should be left for the future decision of their Lordships whether any and what allowance should be made to the Bank to repay them for the loss".[15] Noting that the question of compensation required "deep consideration", the Lords of the Treasury agreed to reserve the question.

The Bank sold the silver coin at its market price to the mint; that is, silver coin which they had accepted for 5/6d was sold to the mint for less than 5/–. But two years later, when the Bank wished to increase its supply of silver coin, they argued that they should not have to pay the official value (5/6d per ounce) for the coins. The Bank accompanied its request with a not-so-subtle threat:

> Should Lord Althorp not deem it expedient to adopt that course or to take any other measure for discharging the debt now due to the Bank, and at the same time to relieve them from future responsibility, The Court request the Governor and Deputy Governor respectfully to represent that they must decline the general receipt of Silver further than may suit their own convenience; and the Court will from time to time apply to the Master of His Majesty's Mint for any supplies of silver coin which they may require for the use of the public.[16]

Their lordships replied to the Bank's threat by stating that they could not give the Bank special privileges with respect to the price at which they bought and sold silver;

[15] T1: 3141/6277; 3/3/1831.   [16] MCD: Eb G4/56, p. 218, 5/12/1833.

that they thought that the renewal of the Bank Charter had "cancelled all former claims"; and that if a proposal of the kind the Bank suggested were put to Parliament, "the proposition would be rejected" since

> the melting of the silver coin [in 1831] was adopted at the suggestion and for the convenience of the Bank; – as it was effected at the expense of the public, and as it now appears that this measure was decided upon an erroneous view of what were to be the permanent wants of the public; at least in the extent to which the operation was carried it would not be just to saddle the country with the expense consequent upon this transaction.[17]

The Bank agreed that "so long as the Mint continues to issue silver coin at a seignorage, and the publick are allowed to pay an unlimited amount of that Coin into the Bank at its current value in exchange for Notes or gold; So long will common justice require that the Bank should be allowed to throw back upon the Mint at the same value any excess beyond the fair wants of the publick".[18]

In 1834 a tentative agreement was reached. The mint would coin £600,000 without charging the Bank seignorage, but the Bank would pay the expenses of coining. The Bank agreed so long as it had the right to send in any excess over £250,000.[19] "The Bank shall be at liberty at their discretion to return all silver coin [to the mint at its

[17] MCD: Eb G4/56, p. 255, 2/1/1834.
[18] MCD: Eb G4/56, p. 257, 2/1/1834.
[19] MCD: EB G4/56, p. 281, 18/1/1834.

par value] which they may receive from the Public above a balance to be retained by the Bank of £250,000".[20]

Finally the Bank accepted the terms and in January 1836 sent the mint £600,000 to be coined. The Bank would bear the costs of coining, of loss from wear and tear, and the interest on the deficiency of silver.[21] The monetary authorities had finally learnt that for the silver tokens to circulate at a value in excess of the market value of their silver would require not only limited legal tender and controlled supply but also an agency that would convert them on demand into a money form that was unlimited legal tender.

THE COPPER COINAGE

By the late eighteenth century the copper coinage in England had fallen into a state of chaos. The official coins had mostly been melted down, and the circulating coins were almost all counterfeits. The best copper coins in circulation were privately issued tokens issued by some of the Birmingham machine shops. They issued coins that were carefully stamped, therefore suffering minimally from counterfeiting. This made convertibility into "coin of the realm" feasible, and the coins could therefore be trade at a greater value than their copper content. The most well known were issued by Wilkinson and the Anglesey copper company.

[20] MCT; G8/26, p. 55, 6/3/1833.
[21] MCD: GB G4/58, p. 328, 7/1/1836.

In 1786 Mathew Boulton built a private mint at Soho with the intention of using steam engines produced by Boulton and Watt to add value to the copper from his Cornwall mines. According to Watt, Boulton had first discussed the idea of applying steam power to minting in 1774, and it may have been with that in mind that in 1785 he established the Cornwall copper company to purchase all the output of Cornwall copper mines. Their mint, at Soho near Birmingham, produced copper coins under private contract for the East India Company and other private contractors.

Boulton told the Committee that he would build a press and mint the coins for them, but the Committee ceased meeting after only a few months. Boulton turned to export markets selling coins to Indian states, Sierra Leone and Sumatra and selling mint machinery to Denmark and Russia.[22]

In March 1797 the PCC was reconstituted, and again determined to reform the copper coinage. After hearing from the Chas. Wyatt Company (who made pennies for Wilkinson and the Anglesea Co.) and Westwood (who made Provincial tokens) the Committee asked Boulton to provide some proofs. Boulton supplied some, noting that since his penny "cannot be perfectly imitated but by the operation of great and expensive machines, it is not likely that it should be counterfeited in any dangerous extent".[23]

---

[22] Challis (1992: 447). The sale of the mint to Catherine the Great of Russia was permitted by (39 Geo. 3 c96), (Doty, 1993: 171).

[23] BT6-126: 70; 28/3/1797. The moneyers at the mint also desired to provide the copper coinage but the Committee noted the precedents of 1693 and 1695 for contracting out the copper coinage (BT6-126: 74; 28/3/1797).

Boulton continued noting that his coin "is much more difficult to be counterfeited than any money ever put into circulation in Europe". The coins would be struck in steel collars so that each coin would be exactly round and of uniform diameter, while indenting the inscription would make the coin more durable.[24]

The Committee gave Boulton a contract to produce 480 tons of pennies and 20 tons of twopenny pieces to be coined at 16d per pound. The size of the coins led to their "cartwheel" nickname. In July the coins were proclaimed to be legal tender up to 1 shilling in value. A minute of the meeting notes that "As the penny and twopenny piece will have an intrinsic value (workmanship included) equal to their nominal value, Ld. L [Lord Liverpool] thinks it will be right to make them legal tender for a shilling especially as this regulation would have a tendency to drive the very bad sixpences out of circulation".[25]

While the Committee thought that the halfpennies were in highest demand, they decided to coin pennies and twopenny pieces first for fear that a coinage of the halfpennies would drive out the old coin, and hurt the labouring poor – presumably because the bad coins then in the hands of the poor would no longer be accepted (BT6-127; 229). Two further contracts for pennies and twopenny pieces were given, but Boulton continued to press for a coinage of halfpennies and farthings. Writing to the Committee in 1797 he stated: "I am fully persuaded from the tendency of all the letters I have received and from the general Voice of the Country that it will be found necessary to coin a quantity of halfpennies and far-

---

[24] BT6-126: 77; 28/3/1797.   [25] BT6-117: 39; 22/6/1797.

things".[26] In 1799 he received a contract for 550 tons of
halfpennies and farthings to be coined at the rate of 18d
per pound, the increase reflecting the increased price of
copper and the higher cost of making twice as many coins
per pound.

The rise in the price of copper (a product of the inflation and naval demands associated with the Napoleonic
Wars) continued, with the predictable result that the cartwheel coins became undervalued. The coinage of copper
was not "free" in the sense that the mint promised to coin
it on demand at a fixed price. Therefore, if the market price
of copper fell below the mint price, there would not be a
flood of copper coin. One side of the bimetallic knife edge
had been eliminated, but the other side of the knife-edge
could not be avoided: if the price of copper rose above the
mint equivalent of the coins they would be melted down
(or exported, but melting down was the more likely fate
for the heavy metal). By 1805 war-time demand for copper
had pushed the price up to more than 20d per pound:

> A number of persons in trade, many of whom are
> in respectability and in a great line of business,
> have for some time past, and are now in the prac-
> tice of getting into their possession considerable
> quantities of the good Copper Coin, for which they
> give a premium, namely a guinea for every 20/–
> worth and more particularly for the penny pieces
> and halfpence coined by Mr. Boulton, which
> copper money is afterwards sold to Dealers in
> copper and melted. The inducement to this

---

[26] BT6-129: 18/9/1797.

practice is the present extraordinary high price of copper – the same being as high as 20 pence half-penny per pound weight and 16 of the penny pieces only weighing that weight – the profit therefore obtained is readily perceived.[27]

The result was that Boulton's copper coins were removed from the circulation and the situation reverted to that before 1797.

The PCC again received requests for a new supply of copper coin.[28] In 1805 a magistrate in Worcester wrote to the secretary of state concerning the shortage of coins in his area: "In some Cases the Expedient of paying two or more Workmen with one note has been resorted to. In others the masters have been obliged to postpone the payment of their men for two or three weeks".[29] The mint moneyers argued that they had an exclusive right to coin, but Boulton again won the contract.[30] Between 1805 and 1807 Boulton received contracts to mint 1,800 tons of pennies, halfpennies and farthings at the rate of 24d per pound.

Interestingly, the old copper coinage had never been demonetized. Both Boulton and the PCC believed an inverted form of Gresham's Law: that the good coin would drive out the bad.[31] Boulton's view is most emphatically

---

[27] BT6-120: 35; 20/4/1805.   [28] BT6-127: 273, 274.

[29] BT6-120: 21; 7/2/1805.   [30] BT6-127: 279.

[31] For the view of the PCC, see the previous discussion of issuing pennies before halfpennies and also Sir Joseph Bank's comment in 1808 that Lord Liverpool had never agreed to call in the old copper since he believed that if left to their Fate they would be driven out of circulation.

put in a reply to a letter from the PCC that discussed complaints by the London traders of an excess supply of copper.

> The Predilection of the Public for the New Copper Coin is founded upon real and solid advantages. Where the option is between a Coin perfect in its execution so as to leave no doubt as to its legality, and one the legality of which, from its various defects is questionable, and of one with less intrinsic value, the choice will not be doubtful. In any other article of manufacture the result of such a competition would unquestionably be favorable to that, which contained the requisites of greater cheapness and perfection, and still more so do I conceive that this would be the consequence of such a competition between two currencies. . . . The suppression of copper money of every other description in the greater part of the Kingdom has been effected solely by this preference of the Public without the aid of any legislative interference.[32]

He suggests that the old coin has been brought from the rest of the country, where it is no longer accepted, to London.

But the tradesmen in London were not satisfied with this. While the coins were (limited) legal tender and were made in limited quantities under government contract, they were not convertible. The coins were delivered to

---

[32] BT6-121: 39; 5/5/1808.

those wishing them free on board (Boulton included £5 per ton in the manufacturing costs to cover delivery) and were supplied primarily to almshouses and to manufacturers with large wage bills. But, they ended up in the hands of the distillers, brewers and retailers who received them in payments. Yet because of the limited legal tender law they could not pay their wholesale bills in copper, and they sent numerous complaints to both Boulton and the PCC.

In May 1808 representatives of Mr. Whitbread's House stated that "the Partnership had now on hand, after having paid up all their Men's Wages, copper coin to the Amount of £1,800, besides what was expected to come in to the Amount of £400 or £600 more, all of which is the coinage of Mr. Boulton". Boulton's agent, Woodward, told the Committee that "Mr. Boulton never issues any copper coin but according to the actual demands made for the same from time to time".[33]

The Committee decided that Boulton should allow the distillers and brewers to supply London for a while. Boulton replied that he had only been able to increase the circulation by promising a steady supply to those who were switching from alternative sources of copper. After describing the benefits of his coinage (see above) he suggested that "the revulsion of the copper coin of various descriptions which is now in circulation and progressively superceded by the introduction of the new, must be felt before that a sufficient motive can exist for the holders retain and wholly withdraw it from circulation".[34] However, he agreed to assist in recirculating his copper

[33] BT6-127: 492–3; 20/5/1808.   [34] BT6-121: 39; 5/5/1808.

coins, and, in February 1809 Woodward was able to report to the Committee that he had "received from the Brewers who complained of the Oppressive load of copper coin, All that they have been willing to supply me with, being to the amount of nearly £10,000, which I have redelivered to such persons requiring change".[35]

The complaints of too much copper and of the circulation of the old and spurious coins had led to proposals in 1808 to call in the old (i.e., pre-Boulton) coin, and in July 1809 an Order in Council to do so was drawn up. However, "from some circumstances which subsequently occurred it was thought advisable that the said order should not be acted upon",[36] and the matter sat in abeyance until 1813.

In March 1813 the Wholesale and Retail Traders of London called on the PCC and petitioned that the old copper coin be demonetized. In March 1814 they (with the Manufacturers, Mechanics, Brewers, Distillers and Licensed Victuallers in London and its vicinity) memorialized the PCC: they said that the old copper had been rejected everywhere in the Country and was now "confined within the Metropolis, which is the only place it has a free circulation". They complained that (1) they could not pay their debts since all their cash was in copper, (2) they had to buy inferior goods since they could only pay with old copper – or had to pay a premium; (3) they had to be constantly collecting and packing up the copper; (4) the quantity of counterfeit coin was increasing – while they had "rarely seen any attempt to imitate or counterfeit the New Coin". They admitted that they could just refuse to

[35] BT6-119: 9; 23/2/1809. [36] BT6-128A: 233; 19/1/1814.

accept the old Coin but "a fear of offending their Customers and the loss sustained from returning base copper by Servants and Others, a circumstance which is very frequently forgotten, soon induces Tradesmen to relax in their exertions to remedy the growing evil".[37]

The wholesalers volunteered to bag the coin and sell it to the mint in amounts of ten bags of 56 pounds[38] and in January 1814 the government finally acceded to these requests and demonetized and called in the old (pre-1797) copper coin. There were occasional requests for a further supply of copper coin before 1821, but the PCC argued that there was no net shortage. Indeed, in 1857 it was estimated that half of the copper coins in circulation originated in the Boulton issues of 1797–1808. By 1821, the mint had been refurbished and equipped with Boulton's machines and so it resumed the copper coinage, producing pennies and their fractions under warrant from the Treasury.[39]

CONCLUSIONS

The date at which Britain adopted the gold standard is hard to pin down. Some date the gold standard from 1717 when Newton "inadvertently" overvalued gold, causing

---

[37] BT6-124: 40b; 12/3/1814.   [38] BT6-125: 3; 23/12/1813.

[39] The fractional coinage continued at the Royal Mint until 1861 when copper coins were replaced with bronze, and the need for a vast coinage again led to the use of the Boulton and Watt mint (Peck, 1972: 416).

the exodus of silver coinage and a de facto gold standard.[40] Historians typically use 1816, based on the passage of legislation permitting the minting of silver coins with less than the traditional 7.8 grains of silver. However, in 1816, Bank of England notes were inconvertible, and so an alternative dating is 1819 when convertibility in fact resumed, or even 1821 when it was required by law. Finally, 1774 is a possible dating since in that year the legal tender of silver coins was limited to payments of less than £25,[41] and the right to sell silver to the mint (which of course had barely been availed of for some 60 years) was removed. Yet, this was clearly perceived as a temporary strategy reflecting the poor state of the current silver coinage, rather than a determination that silver would never again be unlimited legal tender. In 1777 the mint assayer was sent to France to learn how to coin large amounts of silver, and numerous proposals for depreciating the silver coinage and thereby restoring bimetallism were studied by the mint (Craig, 1953: 248).

The early nineteenth century saw radical changes in methods of coining and in the monetary regime in England. Boulton and Watt won a contract to mint copper pence, halfpennies and farthings, and then sold the mint process to the Royal Mint. At the same time the Exchequer, which had partially demonetized silver in 1774 by making silver limited legal tender, reduced silver to a token coinage. Britain, which had been more or less on a

---

[40] With this interpretation – that overvaluation led to a de facto gold standard – readers should recall that such an argument requires that agents could not use silver at a premium.

[41] Although note this was approximately the annual wage earnings of a labourer in 1774 (Brown and Hopkins, 1981: 12).

de facto gold standard since 1717, adopted a de jure gold standard with the termination of the free coinage of silver in 1798. Yet the coinage had improved sufficiently that the silver token coinage suffered minimal counterfeiting and the modern monetary era began.

A feasible token coinage did not imply the international gold standard in all its ambiguous glory. Firstly, it facilitated monometallism rather than specifically gold or silver monometallism. The adoption of the gold standard reflected England's historical overvaluation of gold and perhaps the ties with Brazil, a leading source of gold. In addition, the sense that a nation on the gold standard was more economically developed or richer may have been influential then, as for later adherents to the gold standard (Gallarotti, 1993). Finally, to be on a silver standard might have made sense if bank notes were a substitute for high-denomination coins, but bank notes were still only issued in denominations of £5 and more in the early nineteenth century. Gold played an important international role through the nineteenth century, and since token coinages rely on the domestic legal tender legislation, they are not as suitable for media of exchange used in international exchange, as the example of the Latin Monetary Union described in the following chapter illustrates.

6

Transition to the
Gold Standard in France

Transition to the Gold Standard in France

While Britain had adopted the gold standard in the early nineteenth century, bimetallism persisted in the rest of Europe until at least the middle of the century. In France the revolutionary republicans engaged in an intense debate about the appropriate monetary regime before reverting to bimetallism in 1803, the famous franc germinal. Yet by midcentury, monetary difficulties led to a reopening of the debate, and in 1865 token silver coins were introduced. In 1866 France, together with Switzerland, Belgium and Italy, established the Latin Monetary Union (LMU) to manage an international token currency circulation. From the mid 1860s the LMU countries were on a de facto gold standard, which became de jure in the late 1870s when market forces would have generated a return to bimetallism or a silver standard.

The history of French coinage in the nineteenth century illustrates the central arguments of this book. The debate in the early days of the Republic, over what monetary standard to adopt, demonstrated that policymakers believed that the bimetallic standard should be adopted because there was a need for gold and silver coins in the medium of exchange and that this required that both should be legal tender in the same unit of account. The modernization of the mint in the midcentury and subsequent introduction of token silver coins and cessation of free coinage of silver highlight the connection between technology and bimetallism. Finally, the troubled history of the LMU shows the international ramifications of abandoning full-bodied currency.

Bimetallism

The first attempts by the postrevolutionary government to reform the monetary system occurred in 1790 when Gabriel de Cussy, a former mint master at Caen, proposed the establishment of a Committee on Coins to the Legislative Assembly.[1] The deputies instructed the Committee to address the problem of a shortage of small-denomination coins, but Cussy determined to use it to undo the 1785 reform. That reform, which had reduced the weight of the gold louis, had raised the mint ratio from 14.5 to 15.5. The reform had engendered considerable debate between those who felt that it was necessary to adjust the coinage to the market gold:silver ratio, and to take account of the effects of wear on the gold coins, some of which had been put into circulation in the 1720s, and those who thought that it was simply an attempt by the Crown to ease its financial problems by generating seignorage revenue.

De Cussy's principal advisors were two men who had been outspoken opponents of the 1785 reform, Véron de Fortbonnais and Angot des Rotours. The Committee generated two reports which argued that silver was the standard of value in France but did not go so far as recommending the demonetization of gold coins. Instead they argued that the gold louis, then valued at 24 livres tournois, should be permitted to fluctuate in value with the market price of gold, but with a legal minimum of 23 livres. The Committee viewed their proposal as a way of eliminat-

---

[1] The Comité des monnaies could be translated as Mint Committee or Money Committee. The ensuing discussion draws heavily on Thuillier (1983: 155–83).

ing the overvaluation of gold (since the mint ratio at 23lt would be 1 : 14.7) without demonetizing gold or requiring a recoinage. Thuillier (1983: 198) argued that the Committee's proposals represented the first attempt to demonetize gold coins and let their value be market determined, but it was in fact no different from the existing situation. Only elimination of the minimum would eliminate the bimetallic regime (or maintenance of a minimum that had a very low probability of being a binding constraint).

Mirabeau, who had been an advocate for the 1785 reform, attacked both the report and its framers with his customary skill. He argued that it made no sense to give a minimum value and that gold coins should be minted but not given any official value. Other opponents to the reports believed that the minimum would become the de facto value, which would imply a reduction in the value of their money holdings. The Legislature tabled the proposals and asked the Committee to return to its stated mission of recommending improvements for the billon coinage. No legislation was passed by the Assembly and France degenerated into monetary and political chaos.[2]

In 1795 the Convention introduced a series of reforms. They attempted to control the assignats; they introduced the metric system and named the units – gram, liter, stere

---

[2] The assignats first issued in 1789 still traded near par in 1793. By mid 1795 they were virtually worthless – primarily because of extensive forgery. Del Mar (1867: 257) reports that "At this period no less than seventeen establishments employing 400 workmen were in operation in London, forging assignats for exportation to France; and we are informed that this was done with such skill that detection was impossible".

and franc (18 germinal an III – 7 April 1795);[3] and, a few months later (28 thermidor an III – 15 August 1795) they implemented Mirabeau's system: the franc was to be a 5 gram (90% fine) silver coin and a 10 gram (90% fine) gold coin would be minted but not valued. Over the next few years, some silver 5 franc coins but no gold coins were minted, and worn and counterfeit coins of the Ancien Regime continued to form the majority of the circulation.

In 1798 the Directorate argued that the failure to value the gold coin had effectively demonetized gold and had resulted in a dearth of gold mint output. They recommended to the Council of 500 (the lower house) that a gold coin of 32 francs be minted. Prieur, the head of the Council's Commission of Finance, rejected this suggestion on the grounds that it represented an attempt to fix a ratio between gold and silver, which was impossible. He argued that in a choice between fixing the weight of the gold coin and letting its value fluctuate or fixing its value and periodically altering the weight, the former was unanimously preferred.[4] The latter, he argued, being the choice of the Ancien Regime, had led to huge reminting costs and a pretext to hide manipulations of the coinage (with the objective of generating seignorage revenue). He proposed instead a law identical to that of 1795 except that for payments of taxes, the value of gold coins would be fixed every six months.

The Council rejected this suggestion and forwarded to

---

[3] They also introduced a new decimal calendar in which year (an) I was the year the Republic was established, 1792.
[4] Prieur (1798: 65).

the Council of Ancients[5] (the upper house) a bill replicating that of 1795, with an addendum stating that the valuation of gold coins would be considered in the future. The Council of Ancients vetoed the bill, saying that it was necessary to state the value of gold coins for all payments (not just receipts of the Treasury), to prevent the necessity of debating the value of money at each transaction.[6] They recommended that the value be set annually, based on the value of gold in the principal nations of Europe. Since they had no power to amend the bill, it was returned to the Council of 500, which was subsequently disbanded by the Consuls.

The debate resumed under the consulate in 1801. Gaudin, Minister of Finance, introduced a bill which compromised between bimetallism and silver monometallism. He proposed that gold coins should be given legal tender values and, if the relative values of gold and silver changed, "gold alone should be reminted".[7] Gaudin

---

[5] Eligibility to the Council of Ancients was restricted to those over 40 and married.

[6] "Would one want to keep this indeterminacy, and consider the gold coin a commodity with weight and fineness certified by the Mint? But then it won't be real money anymore. Without a legal value how could someone be compelled to take it? Won't each transaction in gold coin have to be confirmed? Won't every deal transacted in gold coins cause a double debate, one to determine the price of the good and one to determine the value of the coins. . . . Don't forget that the most important trade, that of agriculture, is almost all done in gold; it is gold that dominates payments in fairs and markets; and while it may serve the vile passion of hoarders it is also put into active circulation when it is used to buy grains and animals" (Cretet, 1798: 103).

[7] In summing up his proposal, Gaudin (1801: 145) stated that it "would fix forever the price and value of silver. . . . Neither its abundance nor

argued that allowing the value of gold coins to float would force people to make intricate calculations and to hold a considerable amount of small change.[8] This, he argued, could not be justified by the need to prevent recoinages when the market ratio changed, because recoinage would only be necessary once every fifty years and would cost the State nothing and individuals little.[9] Gaudin's proposal was met by the traditional opposition in the State Council. Berenger told the State Council that it would result in repeated recoinages: "The inconvenience and expense of a general recoinage will doubtless be sufficient to reject such a proposition".[10] He noted (p. 178) that between 1602 and 1773 the mint price of either silver or gold had been changed twenty-six times. Gaudin in turn responded that to leave the value of gold coin to fluctuate was equivalent to demonetizing all the gold coin in the

its scarcity will ever change the weight, fineness or value of the franc. No-one will be liable to being repaid with less value than they lent. If ever events force a change in the ratio [of 1 : 15.5] only gold will be recoined".

[8] Gaudin (1801: 117).

[9] Gaudin based this conclusion on the non-necessity of a recoinage between 1726 and 1785. Chevalier (1859: 169) notes that this is surprisingly weak logic since there is no reason that historic events should be repeated. He adds that concurrent circulation of gold and silver in fact "ceased a few years after 1803; and 25 years later there was only silver". See below.

[10] Bérenger (1802: 162). He continues: "Of all policies, this is the one most contradictory with logic, because added to an uncertain value is uncertain weight. This destroys the ratio we want, with reason, to establish between the monetary system and the system of weights and measures; all so we can have 20 franc and 40 franc coins whose real value will change the day after they are minted and will have to be immediately reminted to satisfy the intent of the Minister".

country. Since gold made up one-third of the money stock of France, this would impose too much of a reduction in the circulation.[11]

Gaudin's original proposal had carefully legislated the different roles that he envisioned for gold and silver coins. The first article stated that "silver will be the base of the coins of the French republic," and the sixth article stated "the proportion of gold to silver will be 1 : 15.5. If circumstances force a change the gold coins will be reminted".[12] Yet, the final Act was more ambiguous: in the preamble, the "superior" role for silver was clear: "Five grams of silver, 90% fine, constitutes the monetary unit and is named the franc". However, coins of silver and gold were treated symmetrically in the remainder of the legislation.

To sum up: France in 1803 adopted a bimetallic standard despite fears that changes in the market relative price of gold and silver would cause a cessation of concurrent (par) circulation of gold and silver coins and consequent need for an alteration of the coin ratio.[13] Gaudin had intended that such an alteration would be effected by a change in the value of gold; however, the symmetric treatment of gold and silver in the legislation suggested a reversion to

---

[11] This is very similar to Hamilton's justification for recommending a bimetallic standard for the United States in 1791. See Chapter 7.

[12] Chevalier (1859) details the changes in the various drafts of the legislation which were destroyed by the 1871 fire in the Archives of the Minister of Finance (Thuillier, 1983: 63).

[13] Interestingly no-one argued, as the international bimetallists did so vehemently seventy years later, that France could fix the market price by virtue of her size. See, for example, de Laveleye (1891) and Cernuschi (1887).

the traditional response of raising the value of the under-valued metal.

COINING TECHNOLOGY

In 1816 the Royal Mint commenced use of the steam-powered mint machines built by Boulton and Watt. As noted in Chapter 5, this technology was first used on the copper coins produced on contract for the Royal Mint and was then bought by that Mint for use on the gold coins and the new token silver coins. A key selling point for the technology had been the quality of the coins produced, which made counterfeiting the tokens a difficult and expensive exercise. As noted, the token nature of the coins meant that mere replication of their content would be profitable, so that it became important to have coins whose impression would be difficult to replicate.

Both France and the United States negotiated with Boulton and Watt for contract copper coinages in the 1790s, and their Soho (Birmingham) mint was seen as the cutting-edge technology in both countries.[14] In 1792, Alexis-Marie de Rochon, a mint commissioner from 1787 to 1792, describes Boulton and Watt's double-acting steam engine in discussing potential improvements to the coining

---

[14] No coins were supplied to the United States, but there were coins made for the French revolutionary government, "Which coin was afterwards suppressed by the arbitrary measures of a fresh set of rulers in that unhappy country, to the great loss of the French contractors who nevertheless paid Mr. B honourably" according to Watt's memoir of Boulton reprinted in Dickinson (1937: 206).

174

process.[15] He noted that while the French screw press has been improved, "what I would like is to be able to use a steam engine for power as Boulton and Watt do in Birmingham".[16] Thuillier cites an anonymous report dated 1801 which includes a letter from Boulton documenting the benefits of his mint including labour saving, speed and prevention of counterfeiting.

Rochon insisted that the refusal of the French mint to use Boulton and Watt's presses reflected the bureaucratic structure of the mint.[17] However, Dumas in his 1868 history of the French mint suggests that the technology, while known, was unavailable. Dumas – one-time master of the Rouen mint – argued that Boulton and Watt's Soho mint was not open to the public and documents this with an anecdote concerning Watt's refusal to allow Nelson to visit. (Watt's response to Nelson being "Milord, I can't respond [favourably] to your request, but I am glad you asked".) According to Dumas, "No-one would be surprised to find closed a door that wasn't opened for Nelson".[18] While keeping the door shut may have protected Boulton and Watt's intellectual property rights, it does not explain why the French did not buy a mint from Boulton and Watt. Although the export of such machinery was banned until 1843, Boulton and Watt did get Acts of Parliament to permit the sale of mints to Russia and Denmark.[19] Admittedly sales to France might have been more controversial.

Further evidence for the argument that the mint

[15] Rochon (1792: xiv).   [16] Rochon (n.d.: 297).
[17] Rochon (n.d.: 104).   [18] Dumas (1856: 36–7).
[19] The Act for Russia specified Matthew Boulton (39 Geo 3 c 96; 12 July 1799); acts were passed permitting export of mint machinery to

administration delayed technological diffusion can be found in the delay in introducing steam engines for driving the rolling presses of the Paris mint. These were finally purchased in 1807, eleven years after they were first tested. A delay that the inventor, and subsequent authors, attributed to the "bad will and disinterest [of the mint employees]".[20] Similarly, when Jean-Pierre Collot, director of the Paris mint, attempted to buy two steam engines for driving the mint presses and invited, at his own expense, an engineer from the London mint to draw up plans for mint renovations, the administration was uninterested.[21]

The mint finally modernized in the 1830s when, in the face of numerous complaints about the state of the small-denomination coins, the government proposed a new copper coinage. The counterfeiting of the copper coins, the multiplicity of denominations (since many predated the Revolution) and the inconvenience of the heavy larger denominations led to continual complaint: "Every government for thirty years [1817–47] worked to replace them [the copper coins]. Since 1817 serious proposals were taken to government councils. In 1828 the chambers of commerce were surveyed".[22] However, action on the copper coinage had to wait until after the recoinage of the duodecimal (that is, prerevolutionary) gold and silver coinage, which finally occurred between 1829 and 1835.

In 1838 the minister of finance established a commission of inquiry into how to proceed with recoining the

Denmark (44 Geo 3 c 70; 10 July 1804) and Brazil (50 Geo III c63; June 1810) without naming a particular exporter.

[20] Babut (1907: 7). See also Darnis (1988: 148) who argues that the empire rarely favoured metallurgy and mechanics.

[21] Thuillier (1983: 278).   [22] Costes (1885: 103).

copper and billon. The commissioners noted that France had the worst struck coins in Europe, which provided an incentive for counterfeiting. They recommended that the regional mints (of which there were seven) be closed and that the new coins be tokens "as there would be no danger of counterfeiting if one employed good dies and struck them with a machine more powerful than the screw press, to make a clean deep print".[23] They referred to the example of English pennies, whose intrinsic value was only 44% of their face value, to illustrate the possibility.

The link between mint equipment and token coins was similarly emphasized in a report to the House of Deputies in 1841. After a bill was introduced recommending demonetization of the existing billon and copper, the House appointed a Committee, chaired by Pouillet, to examine methods of recoinage. The committee made extensive recommendations, beginning with mint renovations.[24] Pouillet went "from surprise to surprise" in a tour of the Paris mint, where horses were still used for power and the coining presses were screw presses powered by between six and twelve men swinging a beam. Pouillet noted the contrast with the more advanced techniques of the English and German mints and recommended that new powerful machinery with special dies should be used for the tokens to prevent imitation: "perfection of manufacture" is essential for tokens, as it is the only guarantee

---

[23] *Journal des débats*, 16 November 1839. Dumas-Colmont report; Report à M le ministre des finances sur la refonte, Bibliotheque nationale. Lf [158] 47, December 1838.

[24] "The need to retire the bad coin was recognized but it was recognized that it was impossible to make better coins without putting the mints on a better foundation". (Say, 1843: 372).

against counterfeiting. In addition he proposed that the new coinage should be bronze not copper (since the new electrochemistry made pure metals "as easy as leather to work with" and counterfeit) and insisted that the government must stand willing to freely convert the tokens into silver coin.

The inquiries, and imminent recoinage of the copper, gave urgency to the adoption of steam-driven coining presses, which had been under consideration since the early 1830s. The major proponent of these presses was a French engineer, Thonnelier, who had modified the lever press developed by the German engineer Uhlhorn in 1829. Thonnelier began urging the Paris mint to purchase his machine in the early 1830s, and in 1840 installed his press at the Paris mint, hoping that the mint would subsequently purchase it (which they finally did in 1845[25]). An 1843 note to the minister of finance stated that the Thonnelier press made coins twice as fast as the old screw-presses, and used 150% less labour. Yet, the minister of finance was not convinced and formed a committee to establish the potential of the press (Pouillet, Saulnier and Montgolfier), which in 1844 confirmed these findings.

In 1842 the government introduced legislation which would demonetize the old copper coins, issue new bronze coins, buy new mint machinery, close the regional mints

---

[25] The mint did agree to buy the press, but an argument raged for several years as to whether the mint should pay the costs of development (about 20,000f) as well as the costs of production (about 25,000f). See the correspondence between Thonnelier and the minister of finance in Serie E. Affaire T. E. 1840–46. "Estimation de la valeur de la presse Thonnelier", Archives of the Paris Mint.

and have the government take over the mint. The mint organization, put in place after the Revolution and maintained essentially until 1880, comprised a central administration, regional mints operated by private entrepreneurs and regional governmental monitors. Under these arrangements, the (private) regional mint directors received the profits from the coinage and were responsible for paying the workers, the maintenance of the machinery and purchases of tools. The central administration supplied the dies *and the coining presses*, as well as monitoring the receipt and disbursement of bullion and coins. The government argued that the introduction of new machinery at all seven mints would be expensive and unnecessary (as shown during the recoinage of the gold and silver). But closure of the regional mints would confer a monopoly on the Paris mint, and therefore the law proposed that the mints should be taken over by the state. Despite approval for each individual article in this omnibus bill, the bill was defeated in 1843 by a vote of 158 to 147.[26]

In 1848 a law proposing the issue of 250,000f of copper was passed, and 44 Thonnelier presses were ordered for the coinage.[27] However, the provisional government of 1848 ignored this law, and it wasn't until 1852 that the new bronze coinage was issued creating a new token coinage of which Dumas wrote in 1868: "The state determined to give to their manufacture a perfection which by

[26] Say (1845: 271).
[27] See letter from Thonnelier to the minister of finance, August 1848, in Serie E. Affaire T. E. 1840–46. Archives of the Paris Mint.

preventing counterfeiting conserved their fiat value; one can be certain that the number of these coins is limited and in keeping with the need".[28]

THE EXPERIENCE OF THE
FRANC GERMINAL

Figure 6.1 shows the relative market price of gold and silver from 1803 to 1873. After the conclusion of the Napoleonic Wars the relative value of gold rose above 15.5 and remained there until 1849. There has been considerable debate both amongst contemporaries and in the recent academic literature about the consequences of this price rise for the French circulation. There are two polar sides of the debate: (1) that the price did not deviate from 15.5 enough to drain all the gold from France, and indeed, that if there were no gold in France the ratio would have been far higher – that is, that France was a "large" economy, and the price of gold was constrained by the mint price plus transactions costs; (2) the price was above the gold export point plus transactions costs, and that by at least 1840 there was virtually no gold circulating in France, with the exception that gold coins could be obtained at a premium.

This is the Gresham's Law debate again. Does Gresham's Law hold, and was gold a "good" money or, more carefully, "good enough" to be driven from circulation? Friedman (1990) has argued that the deviation

---

[28] Dumas (1868: 99).

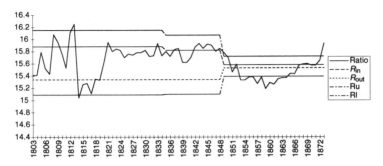

Figure 6.1. Silver: gold ratio. Source: Shaw (1896 [1967]: 159).

between the mint price and the market price was sufficiently small that it would not have been profitable to
export gold and import silver, and more detailed analysis
(below) supports this conclusion. However, the composition of the monetary stock would also be affected by
the metal used to finance balance-of-payments deficits/
surpluses, and even a small difference between the mint
price and market price could create a bias for one metal
in such flows.

If France had a balance-of-payments deficit, a foreign
merchant would choose the metal of payment by comparing the costs in the two metals. Assuming that the relative
price of gold to silver for the foreign merchant is given by
R, he would pay in gold if $R < R_{in}$, where R_{in} is defined
as the relative cost of a livre tournois in each metal.[29]
Similarly, if France had a balance-of-payments deficit, the
French merchant would choose the metal to export for
payment by comparing the costs of the metals in France

---

[29] $R_{in} = (MP_g - c_g)/(MP_s - c_s)$, where MP_i is the mint price in France,
and c_i includes all transportation costs.

(say R_{out}) with their rate in acceptance overseas (R).[30] If $R > R_{out}$, then the merchant would pay in gold.

Figure 6.1 shows estimates of the values of R_{in} and R_{out} compared to Shaw's data on the relative price of gold to silver.[31] The data suggest that until 1850 $R > R_{out}$, so that gold was always exported from France in preference to silver, and during much of that time $R < R_{in}$, so that foreigners would ship gold to France to pay their debts.[32] Trade data suggest that inflows were actually predominantly in silver, suggesting that the R_{in} is slightly overestimated. Evidence from mint output statistics (Figure 6.2) tells a similar story: there is little but not zero gold coinage between 1820 and 1850. Similarly there were numerous statements of contemporaries that there was very little gold in circulation by 1840.[33]

[30] $R_{out} = (ME_g + c_g)/(ME_s + c_s)$ where ME_i is the mint equivalent in France.

[31] Transportation costs are based on Seyd (1879) and brassage rates are taken from the Decimal Coinage Commission Appendix No. 22. I have assumed that the cost of transporting gold is lower (in percentage of value) than that of silver but the conclusions in the text are not altered by assuming that transportation costs were the same for both metals, as suggested in Flandreau (1996: 877).

[32] The main reason for the bias towards gold for both imports and exports was the lower seignorage rate for gold: seignorage rates for gold were 0.29% before 1835 and 0.19% after; for silver they were 1.5% before 1835 and 1% after.

[33] For example the Bank of France commented on the disappearance of gold in 1841, and an economist writing in 1851 stated that "there is scarcely any [gold] left in the country but minimal quantities destined to be pocket money of the rich or reserves for a small number of hoarders". These and other examples are cited in Redish (1995).

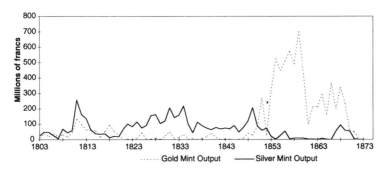

Figure 6.2. French mint output. Source: Willis (1901: 301–7).

The conclusion that Paris had essentially no gold coin circulating at par is consistent with two sources of evidence of gold premia. In 1832 the Bank of England furnished the Committee on the Bank of England charter with weekly prices for the rate of exchange on Paris and the "premium on gold at Paris" for the period 1820–32. This premium fluctuated considerably and ranged from a low of 75c to 16.5f.[34] Stefan Oppers (1994) used the prices of bills of foreign exchange to estimate the proportion of gold and silver that a rational agent would expect to receive in payment of a bill of exchange drawn on Paris. Prices in 1848 were consistent with Parisian bills being paid solely in silver (or in gold valued at its market price rather than at its lower face value).

The falling share of gold in French circulation generated little response, with the exception that the Bank of France

---

[34] P.P. 1831–2, Report of the Committee on the Bank of England charter. Appendix No. 97; reprinted in IUP Series of B.P.P. Monetary Policy, General, Vol. 4.

183

petitioned to be allowed to issue notes of denomination smaller than its existing minimum of 500f, in order to provide a high-value medium of exchange.[35]

The monetary situation changed in the 1850s with the fall in the price of gold. From 1853 to 1866 gold was over-valued by the mint, and the debate about the operation of Gresham's Law was replayed. The gap between the market ratio and mint ratio widened sufficiently for bimetallic arbitrage (the export of silver to purchase gold for coining) to become profitable. Figure 6.1 shows estimates of the bounds for profitable bimetallic arbitrage as R_u and R_l. If the relative price exceeded R_u then it would pay an agent to export gold from France to buy silver, while if it fell below R_l, then it would pay to export silver from France to buy gold.[36]

The figure shows that bimetallic arbitrage was very rarely profitable before the 1850s,[37] but that silver exports for gold would have been profitable from 1851–64. Trade data are not very reliable but are consistent with bimetallic arbitrage in the 1850s. Willis (1901) states that silver

---

[35] Banque de France, "Compte Rendu pour l'exercise 1841", in *Journal des économistes* Vol. 1, p. 322. The Bank argued in favour of notes of 250f and 100f to avoid the difficulty of transporting silver, and to substitute for gold which "disparaît de plus en plus de la circulation". In 1847 the bank was permitted to issue 200f notes.

[36] Several factors combined to narrow the specie points relative to the 1840s: transportation costs within France and between France and Britain fell with the introduction of railways; minting costs fell with better minting technology. See Chapter 2 for definitions of R_u and R_l.

[37] Marc Flandreau (1995) carefully calculated the costs of trading in the precious metals, and took account of the costs of transporting gold to Paris from different parts of France. He suggests that there was a

coin valued at 1.465 billion francs was exported between 1853 and 1860 while 3.082 billion francs of gold coin was imported.[38] Evidence from mint output statistics shows very high levels of silver coinage from 1853 to 1860 and still high levels until 1870. Gold mint output was zero from 1857 to 1867.

Further evidence that the drain of silver occurred through bimetallic arbitrage rather than simply through the balance-of-payments channel is the speed of the transition. Flandreau concludes that Paris was emptied of silver by 1853, and Nantes and Marseilles by 1857. In 1854 de Molinari, an economist writing in the *Journal des économistes*, commented that "The circulation is today literally invaded by gold coin. Silver coin has disappeared, in contrast, and already it is necessary to pay a premium of 1 or 2 percent to get any".[39] A year later Henri Baudrillard stated that "silver has disappeared".[40] In 1859, Chevalier reported "Not only is much less silver coined [since 1853] but even that which the country possessed has been rapidly disappearing".[41] The Monetary Commission held in 1869 concluded that by the end of the 1850s silver represented no more than 2 or 3 percent of the circulation.[42]

---

premium on gold in Paris (i.e., a lack of gold coins circulating at par) at the same time that gold circulated at par in the more remote areas of the country.

[38] Flandreau (1995: 337) estimates the stocks of silver and gold coin in France in 1850 to have been 2.36 billion francs and 0.84 billion francs, respectively.

[39] de Molinari (1854: 211).   [40] Baudrillard (1865: 360).

[41] Chevalier (1859: 47).   [42] Thuillier (1983: 330).

INTRODUCTION OF TOKEN SILVER COINS

The scarcity of silver in the 1850s occasioned a much quicker reaction than the scarcity of gold in the 1840s. Writing in the *Économiste Français*, economist de Molinari noted: "the scarcity [of gold] didn't, in all honesty, cause much inconvenience. Undoubtedly, gold coins are, for many transactions, preferable to silver, but if necessary, one can do without them; silver and bank notes can take their place. . . . [The abundance of gold presents] much greater inconvenience than did its scarcity".[43]

The first complaints of a lack of "change" were heard in 1850. The minister of finance responded by establishing a commission to examine questions related to bimetallism.[44] The Commission concluded that the fall in the value of gold might be temporary, and that a response would be inappropriate. However, the government did begin issuing 5 franc gold coins in 1854.[45]

Through the mid-1850s the question of the appropriate response to the influx of gold occupied economists and politicians. The *Journal des économistes* published the debate of the Political Economy Society in January 1854, on the topic of whether or not to abandon bimetallism. Chevalier, Parieu, Garnier and Wolowski were amongst those proposing such solutions as the recoinage of gold, the demonetization of silver and the maintenance of the status quo.

---

[43] de Molinari (1854: 210).   [44] Baudrillard (1865: 362).
[45] "This coin, so inconvenient because of its dimensions, has become very abundant in France, following the disappearance of virtually all the old silver 5 franc coins". Dumas (1868: 93).

Transition to the Gold Standard in France

In 1857 a second commission was established, again in response to petitions to the government. This commission, instructed to study the monetary situation, considered both the adoption of a gold standard with token silver, and a change in the mint equivalent of gold but opted instead to recommend a tax on silver exports. The government rejected this recommendation on the grounds that it was contrary to "true economic principles".[46]

Meanwhile monetary reform in Switzerland provided a model for those calling for reform in France. The Swiss monetary system was, like the French, based on the 5 gram, 90 percent fine silver franc. Although gold coins were not legal tender, they flowed into Switzerland and tended to drive out the silver coin.[47] In January 1860 the Swiss responded to this by making the 20 franc gold coin legal tender and simultaneously issuing token 2 franc, 1 franc and 50 centimes coins: they reduced their fineness from 90 percent silver to 80 percent silver, made them limited legal tender and permitted their issue only on government account.

The new Swiss tokens were identical in size and weight to the 1 franc, 2 franc and 50 centimes pieces of France and Belgium but contained 10 percent less silver. Furthermore

---

[46] See the summary in the "Rapport de la Commission Chargée d'Etudier la Question monétaire" cited in Willis (1901: 14).

[47] "The national and cantonal treasuries can no longer withstand the urgency of circumstances; the gold standard has become matter of fact, whereas the silver standard remains standing only on paper, and one can without exaggeration assume that nine-tenths of all transactions in Switzerland are performed by means of gold, and especially through the agency of the 20 franc coin" (Soetbeer, commenting on the situation of 1859, cited in Willis, 1901: 30).

187

Swiss silver coins were legal tender in France and Belgium and were widely accepted prior to 1860. Not surprisingly, entrepreneurs imported the new coins into France where they were accepted at par.[48]

In 1861 the scarcity of silver coins was again brought to the attention of the French government. A petition to the Senate asked for a remedy for "the total lack of silver coin which renders the payment of unimportant [i.e., small] demands difficult".[49] In May 1861, in response to further petitions, the minister of finance struck a new commission with a more specific mandate: to examine the question of subsidiary silver coins.

The commission recommended reducing the fineness of the silver coins of less than 5 francs to 83.5% from 90%, but again the recommendation fell on deaf ears. However, the Italian government, which faced a similar monetary problem to that of Switzerland and France, did adopt the spirit of these recommendations. The Italian monetary reform of August 1862 introduced the 5 lire (5 gram, 90% fine) silver coin with unlimited legal tender and free coinage, but it also provided for coinage of tokens (83.5% fine) for denominations less than 5 francs. By 1863 "the invasion of the French circulation by new Italian coin had already proceeded sufficiently far to be regarded as an additional danger" (Willis, 1901: 39).

In May 1864 the French government finally implemented some of the recommendations of the 1862 Report, and agreed to issue 50 centimes and 20 centimes tokens

---

[48] In April 1864, the French Treasury prohibited its public offices accepting the Swiss tokens (Fould, 1866: 784).

[49] Willis (1901: 34).

that would be 83.5 percent fine.[50] They argued that the franc was defined as a 5 gram 90 percent fine coin, and that only the subsidiary coinage should be altered.[51] Since the fineness of the 1, 2 and 5 franc coins was not changed, these coins continued to be scarce.

LATIN MONETARY UNION

The introduction of token coins in France had international implications. By 1852 Belgium, Switzerland and Italy had adopted monetary standards based on the *franc germinal* (see Table 6.1). The origins of this monetary uniformity were Napoleonic. In 1798 when French armies invaded the Netherlands and briefly (1810–14) incorporated them into the French empire they also imposed the new French monetary system. In 1816 the Dutch guilder was reestablished in the Netherlands, but when the Belgian provinces revolted and declared independence from the Netherlands in 1830, they reinstituted the French monetary system.

In 1798 French revolutionary armies also invaded Switzerland, where they established the Helvetic

---

[50] This increased the mint equivalent of these coins by 7.8% and thereby lowered the bimetallic arbitrage point from 15.18 to 14.38 making their export unprofitable. The government was only willing to lower the fineness, and make into token coins, the subsidiary coinage, and did not change the fineness of the 1 franc and 5 franc coins.

[51] Similarly, in the United States, the Act of February 21, 1853, only reduced the fineness of the fractional silver coins (Martin, 1973: 841).

Table 6.1. *Coinage of the Latin Countries before the Union*

	France	Belgium	Switzerland	Italy
Date of legislation	7 April 1803	5 June 1832	7 May 1850	24 Aug. 1862
Silver				
Basic coin: value	1 franc	1 franc	1 franc	1 lira
Weight	5 gm.	5 gm.	5 gm.	5 gm.
Fineness	90%	90%	90%	90%
Value/kg fine silver (ME$_s$)	222.2	222.2	222.2	222.2
Mint price/kg fine silver	220.56			220.5
Denominations	5f, 2f, 1f	5f, 2.5f, 1f	5f, 2f, 1f	5f, 2f
	50c, 20c	50c, 20c	50c	
Gold				
Basic coin: value	20f	20f		20 lira
Weight	6.45 gm.	6.45 gm.		6.45 gm.
Fineness	90%	90%		90%
Value/kg fine gold (ME$_g$)	3444.4	3444.4		3444.4
Mint price	3437.0	3437.0		3437.0
Denominations	20f 40f	20f		20f, 40f
Coin ratio: ME$_g$/ME$_s$	15.5	15.5		15.5

Source: Willis (1901: 164).

Republic and again instituted a monetary system based on the franc (Carson, 1970). Between 1803 and 1850 the right to mint coins returned to the individual cantons, who created a currency that was "as motley as it was inconvenient" (Lardy, 1878: 190). After unification in 1848, the power to mint and to define money was reserved to the federal government, which adopted a silver coinage identical in dimension and composition to that of France and Belgium, although it made no allowance for either minting or giving legal tender status to gold coins. In June 1852 the silver coins of France, Belgium and some Italian states were made legal tender.

Napoleon had introduced the franc to Italy also, in 1793, but it was suppressed in 1814. Unification in 1861 led to the creation of a national monetary unit, and again led to the adoption of the French system. The lira weighed 5 grams and was 90 percent fine silver, and the gold:silver ratio was 1:15.5 (Kindleberger, 1984: 137). Coins of Belgium, Switzerland and France were also given legal tender status. The legislation (being passed in 1862, after the fall in the price of gold) also provided for the issue of token silver coins. Consequently, by 1862 the French, Belgian, Italian and Swiss economies all used the same unit of account and gave legal tender status to coins issued by each other.[52] The increase in the relative value of silver therefore led to a shortage of silver coins in all four countries.

By 1865 Belgium was the only country of the four

---

[52] Interestingly, the granting of legal tender status to foreign coins was widespread even amongst countries using different units of account. Thus gold coins of France, Spain and Great Britain were legal tender in the United States until 1857.

without its own token currency and its circulation was virtually devoid of Belgian coin. The tokens of the other three nations circulated widely but were not legal tender. In 1865 the Belgian government called for a convention of the four nations in order to find a communal solution to the problem of the small coins.

The delegates to the convention met six times between November 20 and December 23. De Parieu (vice-president of the French Council of State) opened the conference and concluded his speech with a list of eight questions the convention would address. These (listed in the appendix) all concerned the subsidiary coinage and noticeably excluded the question of abandoning the bimetallic standard for the gold standard. Concern from delegates from other nations, who all advocated adoption of the gold standard, compelled de Parieu to add this issue to the agenda.

The delegates quickly resolved most of the issues. There would be free coinage of gold and each member state would receive at par gold coins minted by the other states. All silver coins less than 5 francs in value were to be token coins. The tokens would be of uniform fineness. Each state could mint up to 6 francs per capita, and the tokens would be legal tender amongst private agents only in payments up to 50 francs. The right to mint tokens was reserved to the government. State treasuries would accept up to 100 francs in the tokens of the other states. Each state stood ready to buy at par with gold or 5f silver coins, their tokens held by treasuries of other states.

The most controversial issues were whether or not to continue the free minting of the 90% fine 5 franc silver coins – that is, to maintain the de jure bimetallic standard

– and what fineness to adopt for the token coins. The delegates of Italy, Belgium and Switzerland all advocated a de jure gold standard, but the French delegation flatly refused such a change.

Prior to 1850 the LMU nations had been on a de facto silver standard and there had been little debate about the merits of the system. There were (prior to the 1850s) two advantages of the silver standard. Moving to a gold standard would be costly, as the silver money stock would have to be replaced with (relatively expensive) gold. Furthermore a gold standard would not provide a small-denomination medium of exchange. By the 1860s these problems had been overcome. The low price of gold had ensured that the majority of the specie money stock was gold, and the token issues, already in use in three of the four nations, showed how a small-denomination medium of exchange could be supplied.

Why then, did the LMU not legislate a gold standard? In the first place there was no immediate need: the monetary systems of all the nations were on a de facto gold standard. Secondly, the delegates from France flatly refused. Two explanations for French behaviour have been proposed: that the Bank of France preferred a bimetallic standard, and Napoleon's fiscal needs required him to accommodate the bank's wishes (Willis, 1901). Secondly, that Napoleon was planning an international monetary conference in 1867 at which he hoped a world monetary standard would be adopted. Napoleon intended to trade his willingness to go from bimetallism to a gold standard in return for that gold standard being based on the French gold coinage (Russell, 1898). The convention finally agreed to continue the free minting of silver 5 franc coins 90% fine, and that they would be received by all the member states.

The fineness of the tokens was an issue because the existing Swiss tokens were 80% fine while those of Italy and France were 83.5% fine. It was finally decided that the larger emissions of 83.5% fine coins (of which 116 million francs had been issued in contrast with 10 million francs in 80% fine coins) made a choice of 83.5% fineness wiser. The Swiss were given twelve years to retire their 80% fine coins. The treaty was ratified in July 1866 and went into force August 1, 1866.

Since Italy, Switzerland and France had unilaterally issued a token coinage, why was a multilateral response required? Why did Belgium suggest such a response and the other nations agree so readily? While the answer is different for specific countries, the bottom line is that each country realized that there were gains from having a uniform numeraire and unit of account.[53] That is, the usefulness of a unit of account increases with the number of agents/transactions that use it. In 1864 each country (except Belgium) had different denominations of tokens and had different finenesses. Many foreign tokens circulated in each country and yet they were not legal tender and were not convertible into gold at par without the costs of transportation to the country of origin. The issue of token coins generated seignorage revenue equal to the

---

[53] Niehans (1978) distinguishes between the numeraire, e.g., silver, and the unit of account, e.g., 5 gms. of 90% fine silver. The LMU countries in 1864 already had the same numeraire and the same unit of account.

difference between the official value of the token and the gold costs of its silver content. For example, the Swiss franc of 1860 contained 4 grams of silver, which in 1860 had a gold value of 90 centimes.[54] Seignorage-maximising behaviour would cause a country to increase its issues which would leak into neighbouring countries exacerbating the problem.[55]

Belgium, Switzerland and Italy also joined the LMU to give themselves a forum to convert France to gold monometallism. While they wished to adopt a gold standard, there were more gains from maintaining a common unit of account with France. Furthermore, in 1865 the point was academic – each country was on a de facto gold standard.

The most frequently cited cause of the institution of the LMU was a desire to expand the bimetallic currency area. For example, Yeager (1976: 296) states that the LMU was established "in hopes of promoting an international standardization of currencies on a bimetallic basis". Kenwood and Lougheed (1971: 119) suggest a similar motivation: "In an effort to stabilize the situation and promote an international bimetallic system, France summoned a meeting of the franc-using nations in 1865". Yet, in 1865 the majority of countries were on a bimetallic standard, and the bimetallic area did not need promotion. The argument that the LMU represented an attempt to institute international bimetallism is, I think, inappropriate or at least anachronistic. The agreement allowed for and encouraged other

---

[54] Since $R = 15.29$ and $ME_g = 3.444$, the gold value of the token 80% fine franc = $((5*0.8)/15.29)*3.444 = 0.9$.

[55] A similar problem was common in the seventeenth century; see Van der Wee (1977).

nations to join, as Greece did in 1867. However, only France of the four countries wished to maintain a de jure bimetallic standard, and there is considerable evidence that this stance (which the de facto gold standard made costless) represented a bargaining chip to be surrendered later, rather than a hard-line philosophical position.

An alternative explanation for the formation of the LMU is that it formed an optimal currency area in the sense of Mundell (1961). This literature on optimal currency areas has analysed the desirability of monetary union (that is a fixed exchange rate) in the twentieth-century world of fiat money systems. The calculus involves trading off the benefits of a reduction in transactions costs implied by a fixed exchange rate against the cost of losing the ability to run an independent monetary policy. In the nineteenth-century world of commodity money standards, the costs and benefits of a monetary union were clearly very different because under a commodity money standard monetary authorities had virtually no control over monetary policy to give up.

A more relevant factor in the emergence of the LMU was the general climate of economic integration in the midnineteenth century. The expansion in international trade is well documented, and reflected transportation improvements, technological and political changes as well as trade liberalization. Examples of the latter include England's move to free trade, Italian and Swiss unification, the formation of the Zollverein and the Cobden-Chevalier Treaty. International expositions provided further evidence of the desire for integration, as did attempts to introduce a uniform system of weights, measures and coinage in Western Europe. The latter is particularly relevant in the context of the LMU. In 1867 a sub-committee of the International Statistics Congress met in Paris and delegates from twenty-two countries (including the United States) voted to establish the gold standard and an international unit of account based on the 5 franc coin.[56] The formation of the LMU was consistent with this background of harmonization. The importance of international trade increased the gains from standardizing the token coinage.

Finally, we can turn to the accomplishments of the LMU. It did institute a token coinage, which was reasonably successful. It did not encourage bimetallism. As shown above, in the early 1860s the LMU countries were on a de facto gold standard. As shown below, when the de jure bimetallic standard might have affected the monetary systems of the member countries they all abrogated the bimetallic standard.

The adverse consequences of the fall in the relative price of gold provided the impetus for the convention of 1865, and the object and accomplishment of the convention was to provide a uniform small-denomination coinage (i.e., token silver). Ironically, the price of gold rose shortly after the convention. However, this did not end the LMU, because the partner countries decided not to return to a de facto silver standard, and because

---

[56] However, a commission established in Britain to consider adoption of the new unit argued that although the benefits of uniformity were significant, they were outweighed by the high costs of establishing a new numeraire and adjusting all contracts written on the basis of the old numeraire. By the 1870s the prospects of an international monetary standard were eliminated by the Franco-Prussian War and subsequent German monetary reform.

in the interim both France and Italy had made bank notes legal tender.

In France the *cours forcé* began in 1870 as a reaction to the Franco-Prussian War. Although the Bank of France did not formally resume convertibility until 1878, the depreciation of the franc was limited especially after the Bank began redeeming its 20 franc notes in gold in 1873 (Willis, 1901: 148). The Italian experience was very different. With brief exceptions the notes of the Banca Nazionale were legal tender between 1866 and 1884, as a result of war- and unification-related fiscal problems. By 1868 the lira had depreciated by 12 percent. This meant that the Italian token coins that were accepted as legal tender in the LMU countries were driven out of domestic circulation and used to pay foreign debts. The Italian government agreed only to redeem repatriated tokens in their paper currency. Termination of the treaty would have left the other nations with stocks of these depreciated tokens, providing a strong motivation for the other three countries to maintain the Treaty.

The other reason for the prolongation of the Treaty was the unwillingness of the LMU nations to return to a de facto silver standard. Since all four countries had been on a de facto gold standard in 1865, the question of the standard had been academic. When the increase in the price of gold in the 1870s threatened to impose a de facto silver standard in the bimetallic LMU nations, immediate action was taken to prevent silver driving the gold coin out of circulation. A series of expedient measures by individual countries and the LMU created a mixed standard, subsequently known as the limping gold standard, under which only gold was freely minted but the existing silver 5 franc coins were unlimited legal tender.

In January 1870 the Italian mint lowered its mint price of silver from 220.5 to 218.8 (Willis, 1901: 130). In September 1873, the French government imposed a daily limit of 250,000 francs for silver coinage, a limit that was reduced to 150,000 francs in November. In October 1873 the Belgian government suspended the free coinage of silver. In November 1873 Switzerland asked France to convene a meeting of the LMU nations so that uniform measures could be taken. The French government agreed to call a convention.

At this conference in January 1874 the Belgian delegates clearly stated their desire for a co-operative response. Although Belgium had suspended domestic silver coinages, foreign silver would displace the gold coin unless a multilateral response was undertaken. The Swiss delegates agreed and suggested formal adoption of the gold standard. The French and Italian delegates preferred to maintain the status quo with the addition of limits to silver coinage. While there was a desire to limit the moneyness of silver coin, the large quantities of 5f coins minted between 1867 and 1873 represented a potential liability to the various governments. That is, the value in gold of these coins was less than 5f. If the coins were to be "tokens" the government would have to stand ready to redeem them at 5f in gold. The problem was exacerbated by the large holdings in Switzerland, Belgium and France of Italian 5 lire coins. If Italy were not included in the new arrangements these countries would take a loss.

On January 31, 1874, the four nations undertook to limit

Bimetallism

Table 6.2. *Uncoordinated Issues of Token Coins*

	France	Belgium	Switzerland	Italy
Date of legislation	24 May 1864		31 Jan. 1860	24 Aug. 1862
Denominations	50c, 20c		2f, 1f, 50c	1f, 50c, 20c
Fineness	83.5%		80%	83.5%
Mint equivalent: ME_t	239.5		250	239.5
Coin ratio: ME_g/ME_t	14.38		13.78	14.38

the quantity of silver 5f pieces each would coin that year (see Table 6.2). The four countries took different paths in creating this coinage. The Belgian, Swiss and Italian governments bought the silver bullion and had it coined on government account, receiving the difference between the market price (in gold) and 5 francs as revenue (Willis, 1901: 151). The French continued to permit free coinage until June 1875, when the Treasury began sales of silver to the mint (Willis, 1901: 159). However, private sales were also permitted. In February 1876 the waiting period was approximately two years and the interest cost (20f) eliminated the difference between the market price (200.6f) and the mint price (222.56f). In August 1876 the government proclaimed legislation suspending the coinage of silver 5f and the reception of bullion for minting. (The law was subsequently continued by a law of 5 January 1878.) In December 1876 the Belgian government similarly suspended its coinage of the 5f piece. The countries then agreed that the annual meetings had served little purpose and readily agreed to coinage limits for 1877 of half those of the previous year. In late 1877 similar restrictions were agreed on for 1878.

In 1878 the LMU countries reconvened. The convention of 1865 expired in 1880, but while the raison d'être of the convention – the problem of subsidiary coinage – had gone, it had left an awkward legacy: the smaller countries could not afford to redeem the large French holdings of their overvalued silver coin. The convention of 1878 slightly increased the limits of the token silver coinage (see Table 6.3) and finally suspended the coinage of the 5f silver coin. Thus the "limping gold standard" was inaugurated: only gold was freely minted; however, the existing 5f silver coins were still unlimited legal tender.[57]

The Latin Monetary Union has been interpreted as a monetary union dedicated to bimetallism. If this were the case it would represent a dead end in the path to the gold standard. In fact, the LMU, to the extent that it was about monetary matters, should be seen as a step toward not away from, the gold standard. As Say (1843) put it, the adoption of the gold standard required that legislators learn how to issue a token currency and this was the raison d'être of the LMU.

The issue of tokens was more complex in the LMU countries than in Britain and the United States because (1) countries were contiguous and therefore international trade in coins could be virtually costless, and (2) the countries had identical full-bodied coins and a history of granting legal tender to each other's currency. These conditions

---

[57] Willis (1901: 183) argues that the real focus of the convention was not the continuation of the token coins or the question of the 5 franc coin, but the measures to be taken with respect to Italy.

Table 6.3. *Silver Coinage Limits (millions of francs)*

	France	Belgium	Switzerland	Italy	Greece[a]
Tokens					
Dec. 1865	239	32	17	141	9
Oct. 1878	240	33	18	170	10.5
5 franc piece					
Jan. 1874	60	12	8	40[a]	
Feb. 1875	75	15	10	50	5
Feb. 1876	54	10.8	7.2	36	12
Feb. 1877	27	5.5	3.6	18	6
Feb. 1878					
Nov. 1878	Coinage of 5 franc pieces suspended.				

[a] Greece joined the union in 1868.
[b] Italy was given an additional 2 million lire limit.

meant that co-operation would generate a superior coinage at relatively low cost.

TECHNOLOGICAL DETERMINISM VS. HISTORICAL ACCIDENT REVISITED

I conclude by addressing a recent version of the "historical accident" theory of the emergence of the international gold standard. Marc Flandreau (1996) formulates his thesis in terms of strategic externalities, path dependence and switching costs. He argues that in the late 1860s the increasing development and integration of the world economy raised the gains to a "single currency" – the strategic externalities. As the LMU and Britain happened

202

to have predominantly gold coinage at the time, "the odds were favourable to gold" – the path dependency. Yet high switching costs for France and Germany (the only costs mentioned for France were the possible losses on the sale of silver) precluded the emergence of the international gold standard in the 1860s. Its eventual emergence in 1878 was the result of Germany being able to afford to switch because of the indemnity that came with winning the Franco-Prussian War, and French determination not to provide a market for surplus German silver.

While all these factors are relevant, they can only be part of the story and, without accepting a purely deterministic view of history, a greater role should be given to underlying forces. The most relevant "accident" was the dominance of gold in the circulation of the LMU countries in the late 1850s and 1860s when the nineteenth-century rash of globalization began. This reduced the switching costs to the point where but for the "accident"? of the Franco-Prussian War a different world gold standard would have emerged in the early 1870s.

Flandreau's arguments that the switching costs were too high for France in the late 1860s is hard to accept. He has estimated (Flandreau, 1995: 337) the stock of silver coin as about 15 percent of the total in 1865–70. Very little would have had to be sold, as silver would still be used for the fractional coinage, which is exactly what France did after 1879 by adopting a limping gold standard. Furthermore, he estimates that the stock of silver coin in France fell by 1 billion francs between 1853 and 1859, without any loss.

The argument that strategic externalities required a monometallic currency and that path dependency favoured the use of gold requires the assumption that bimetallism could not supply those strategic externalities. Yet, as the international bimetallists of the late nineteenth century argued ubiquitously, international bimetallism with each country adopting the same bimetallic ratio could provide the same level of strategic externalities.

Flandreau's argument against technological determinism is that (1) it explains only monometallism not bimetallism, (2) France would have adopted the gold standard in 1830, when the steam coining presses were invented, or 1845, when the Paris mint bought them, if technology were the impediment, and (3) token subsidiary coinage did not preclude bimetallism but could complement it.

The first argument is valid, and the accident that British coinage was already predominantly gold in 1800, and the LMU and Britain were de facto on a gold standard in the 1860s is significant. Yet I would argue that the prestige of gold, as a more highly valued commodity than silver, mattered, as did its superior characteristics for international exchange. Ricardo may have said, "the only objection to the use of silver is its bulk . . . but this objection is entirely removed by the substituting of paper money as a general circulation medium", but paper money was not widely used for international exchange in 1800 or even in 1870.[58]

---

[58] Ricardo as cited in Flandreau (1995: 877). Saint Marc (1983; 37) estimates bank notes and deposits to have been 28% of the money stock in France in 1870. Flandreau argues that from the perspective of international shipments "the two metals were essentially perfect substitutes". This is not supported by his citation of Ricardo but is supported by his evidence on transportation costs for silver and gold, and by the evidence on the acceptability of de facto silver monometallism in France in the 1830s and 1840s.

The delay between the modernisation of the mint in the mid 1840s and the final ban on purchases of silver in 1878 tells us that technology was not the only factor that drove the adoption of the international gold standard. It wasn't sufficient; it may have been necessary. The delay reflected various factors. In the 1840s French bimetallism was de facto silver monometallism, which was not viewed as inefficient (in Flandreau's language, the gains from gold monometallism would have been outweighed by the switching costs). In the 1850s with the influx of gold and resultant scarcity of silver the costs of bimetallism increased. The failure to respond by creating a token silver coinage until 1864 reflects in part a lack of urgency but perhaps more the lack of a consensus across the alternative responses. After 1864 France was on a de facto gold standard and, as I argued earlier, had no compelling reason to ban silver sales until agents wanted to sell silver to the mint.[59]

Without denying that subsidiary coins could have complemented a bimetallic standard – again this was a proposal of the international bimetallists – it is important to remember that bimetallism in the period up to the nineteenth century had been entirely motivated by the need for a medium of exchange that could provide high and low denominations efficiently.

In the late nineteenth century, after the international gold standard was essentially in place, the debate over bimetallism became more complex. The elimination of the

---

[59] The delay between technology, globalisation and monetary homogenisation in nineteenth-century Europe is not clearly more dramatic than in twentieth-century Europe.

original motivation for bimetallism led to the introduction of other justifications both self-serving and socially beneficial. The argument began to revolve around issues of price stability, and the way in which particular classes would be affected by inflation, and the political strength of those, such as the Bank of France, who profited from bimetallic arbitrage.

APPENDIX: AGENDA OF THE CONVENTION OF 1865[60]

1. What inconveniences have arisen from the different subsidiary moneys of the countries?
2. Would it be useful to establish a monetary union to facilitate reciprocal circulation of subsidiary money?
3. Should such a union have identical subsidiary coins or just less diversity than now? What fineness should be adopted in either case?
4. Should the union prescribe the fineness of all coins less than or equal to 4 francs?
5. Should these coins be limited legal tender amongst private agents?
6. Should the governments state a maximum amount of wear before coins must be reminted?
7. What should determine the quantities of issue?
8. Would it be advisable to state that gold coins would be accepted by public treasuries?
9. With respect to the 5f piece, would it be advisable to reconsider the bimetallic standard?

---

[60] Chausserie-Laprée (1911: 17–19).

7

Bimetallism in the
United States

Bimetallism in the United States

Amidst all the embarrassments which have sur-
rounded this subject since the adoption of metallic standards of property, it is remarkable that
Governments have so tenaciously persevered in
the effort to maintain standards of different materials, whose relation it is so difficult to ascertain at
any one time, and is so constantly changing; and
more especially when a simple and certain remedy
is within the reach of all. This remedy is to be found
in the establishment of one standard measure of
property.

– S. D. Ingham, U.S. Secretary of the Treasury,
1830

The history of monetary standards in the United States
reflects the influence of forces that we have seen in action
in England and France but also of idiosyncratic factors.
The story of the initial adoption of bimetallism after the
American Revolution, the subsequent debate over the
effects of overvaluation of one metal, the transition to a
de facto gold standard complemented by token coins and
finally the adoption of a de jure gold standard replicated
the experience of England and, more closely, France. The
primary difference in the history of money in the United
States and Europe involves the role of paper money –
bank notes and fiat money. Yet while the U.S. experience
with paper money and banks influenced the debate about
the monetary standard, the similarity of the monetary
regime with those in Europe suggests that it did not have
a major impact on the outcome.

Bimetallism

This chapter analyzes the factors underlying the U.S. choice of monetary regime and its performance. The literature on this topic is vast, and so here I focus on putting the U.S. choices into an international context, and showing that the choices that were made in the United States had international parallels. The chapter begins by showing how the congressional debates reflected both the problems of bimetallic standards and the influence of paper money options. Then I discuss the technology employed at the mint and how it evolved before presenting data on the performance of bimetallism in the United States. The final section of the chapter analyzes the introduction of token silver coins and the so-called Crime of 1873 – the termination of the free minting of silver and de jure adoption of a gold standard.

DEBATES OVER BIMETALLISM IN THE LATE EIGHTEENTH CENTURY

In the late eighteenth century, the new United States adopted a bimetallic standard after debating the choice of regime both under the Continental Congress and under the Constitution.[1] Then, in the first half of the nineteenth century, the debate revolved around the appropriate level for the mint ratio, culminating in a shift from 15:1, which undervalued gold, to 16:1, which overvalued gold, in 1834.

---

[1] The debate began while the war was ongoing, and the Continental currency, fiat money issued to finance the war of independence, was depreciating dramatically (Ferguson, 1961: 32, 67 et passim).

In 1782 the Continental Congress asked Robert Morris, Superintendent of Finance, to evaluate the foreign coins then in circulation, so that the Continental bills which were payable in "Spanish dollars or the equivalent in gold or silver coin" could be redeemed.[2] Morris took the opportunity to propose a monetary standard for the newly organized United States and recommended a silver monometallic standard. He argued that a bimetallic standard would quickly become de facto monometallic, whereas if a silver standard were adopted, paper money could substitute for the use of gold coin.[3] Thomas Jefferson appended to Morris's proposal a note approving the establishment of a mint and a domestic currency but, without addressing Morris's argument, advocated a bimetallic standard.[4] He argued that the mint ratio should be determined by finding the average market price of gold amongst the country's trade partners and then raising the value of gold slightly.

These recommendations were referred to the Grand Committee of Congress (comprising one representative from each of the thirteen States). This Committee noted that France had a ratio between gold and silver of 15:1, Spain 16:1 and England 15.5:1, and that in the latter two countries, the overvaluation of gold made it the medium of exchange. The Committee concluded that "sundry advantages would arise to us from a system by which silver might become the prevailing money", since silver was

---

[2] Morris's report is reprinted in U.S. Senate (1879: 425–32).

[3] He does not specify whether privately issued paper money or state-issued monies. In the 1780s, seven states emitted paper money (Perkins, 1994: 143).   [4] Perkins (1994: 437–43).

more costly to export and more useful as a metal (U.S. Senate, 1879: 445).

In July 1785, Congress resolved that the unit of account would be the dollar, and in August 1786 further resolved to produce dollars containing 375.64 grains of pure silver (and 50c, 20c and 10c coins in proportion) and $10 gold coins containing 246.268 grains of pure silver.[5] Finally in October 1786 an ordinance was passed establishing a mint, and prescribing coining charges for gold and silver of approximately 2%. The legislation also provided for copper coinage on government account, and copper coins were the only ones to be minted before the legislation was annulled by the passage of the Constitution in 1789.

The new Secretary of the Treasury, Alexander Hamilton, returned to the question of monetary standards in 1790 when Congress asked for a report on the appropriateness of the establishment of a mint. Hamilton began by noting the inconsistency in the earlier legislation which both provided for the silver dollar to be the monetary unit and for coins of gold and silver to be produced and freely coined. Furthermore, he explicitly rejected adopting a silver standard plus paper money, arguing that "bank circulation is desirable, rather as *an auxiliary to*, than as *a substitute for* that of the precious metals [his emphasis]". Comparing the merits of gold and silver monometallism, he opted for gold on the basis that, gold may be said "to have a greater stability than silver; as being of superiour value, less liberties have been taken with it in the regulations of different countries" (Hamilton, 1791:

---

[5] The mint equivalents of (91.6% pure) silver and gold were $14.05 and $214/troy lb, respectively.

576–9). Yet, Hamilton concluded in favour of a bimetallic standard:

> Upon the whole it seems to be most advisable, as has been observed, not to attach the unit exclusively to either of the metals because this cannot be done effectually without destroying the office and character of one of them as Money, and reducing it to the situation of a mere merchandise. To annul the use of either of the metals as Money is to abridge the quantity of circulating medium, and is liable to all the objections which arise from a comparison of the benefits of a full with the evils of a scanty circulation.

Two pages later he added that "General utility will best be promoted by a due proportion of both metals. If gold be most convenient in large payments, silver is best adapted to the more minute and ordinary circulation". He advocated a ratio of 15:1 between gold and silver as being as close as possible to the relative market price of the two metals in Europe.[6]

The Act of 1792 embodied most of Hamilton's recommendations and established bimetallism in the United States. Under the legislation the U.S. mint would coin dollars containing 371.25 grains of fine silver and 44.75

---

[6] Laughlin (1896:16) chastises Hamilton for using the European, rather than the U.S., ratio although he admits that Hamilton selected the appropriate ratio despite the fact that "on a matter of principles he was wholly in error". It seems likely that the European ratio determined that of the United States and so it is hardly surprising that the answer came out the same.

grains of copper alloy. The mint would also coin "eagles" containing 247.5 grains of pure gold and 22.5 grains of silver or copper alloy.[7] The "eagle" was to be legal tender for $10.00.[8] The legislation thus rated gold 15 times more valuable than silver and (in an unprecedented fashion) the legislation specifically provided (Sec. 11) that "the proportional value of gold to silver in all coins which shall by law be current within the United States, shall be as fifteen to one according to quantity in weight, of pure gold to pure silver". Any person could bring gold or silver to the mint (free coinage) and have his or her bullion coined without charge.[9]

Compared to the extensive debate over bimetallism in France, little debate preceded the U.S. decision to adopt a bimetallic standard. This may have reflected the widespread international use of bimetallic standards. It may also have reflected the U.S. fiscal position. As a result of Hamilton's plan to re-fund the national debt, the federal government had debt of about $70 million, estimated to be about one-third of GNP. As Garber (1986) observed, the bimetallic standard made all nominal contracts into

---

[7] The gold coins were 11/12 fine, which was a common choice of standard. All weights are in troy. The fineness of the silver coins was 0.8924, a value different from all known coinages!

[8] A Mr. Williams argued in 1797 that the Congress had been given the power to coin, but that the power to declare something legal tender was reserved to the States. His argument was ignored. Breckinridge (1903: 89).

[9] Typically the coinage took a few days. The legislation provided that, if both parties agreed, the mint could advance the coin for a charge of 0.5%. The mint never used this option before 1837, since there were no funds out of which such advances could be paid.

option contracts. While Hamilton's plan went to great lengths to avoid the appearance of repudiation of any part of the debt, the use of a bimetallic standard, if the option were not correctly priced, could lower the real cost of the debt.[10]

Garber's (1986) study pricing the bimetallic option provides some evidence of undervaluation of the bimetallic option. He first computes the value of the bimetallic option using the fundamentals of the stochastic process driving the gold: silver ratio. Then, using the equality between the price of a bimetallic bond and the price of a gold bond less the value of the option to pay in silver, he computes predicted bimetallic bond prices. For the 1820s, the predicted bond prices are always less than the actual prices, which is consistent with an underpricing of the option. For example, Garber computes the "true" bimetallic option value of a bond in January 1821 to be 13.8. That can be compared to the option value implicit in the U.S. bimetallic bonds. The market price of the War Loan of 1814 in January 1821 was 107, while, from data on gold bond prices in London, the value of a gold bond in January 1821 was 115. Thus we get an implied option price of 8, in contrast to the computed value of 13.8. This methodology is hazardous, although the largest expected bias, that it ignores higher country risk in the United States than in Britain (the source of the gold interest rates), works in the wrong direction: We would expect that U.S. bonds would be lower in price than predicted, not higher. At best the

---

[10] Testimony to the astute nature of the re-funding operation is that the market value of the package that Hamilton put together was well below par.

evidence should be read as being not inconsistent with an underpricing of the option.[11]

The suggestion that a bimetallic standard was intro-duced as a complement to Hamilton's plan to fund the national debt is speculative. Albert Gallatin, President of a New York Bank and former Secretary of the Treasury, writing in 1829 argued that "those fluctuations in the rel-ative value of the two species of coin are a quantity which may be neglected; and is, in fact, never taken into consid-eration at the time of making the contract" (U.S. Senate, 1879: 595).

DEBATES OVER BIMETALLISM IN THE EARLY NINETEENTH CENTURY

The choice of a bimetallic regime, and the mint par of 15, was not challenged until after the War of 1812, and the financial crisis that followed it. In the meantime, the twenty-year charter of the Bank of the United States was not renewed in 1811, but the difficulties of financing the war, and the suspension of convertibility of the bank notes of most of the U.S. banks in 1814, convinced the Congress to charter a new, but very similar institution – commonly called the Second Bank of the United States – in 1816. The following year the commercial banks resumed

---

[11] This argument, it should be noted, cannot be applied to the revisions to bimetallism in 1834. By then, the federal debt had been paid off, and a major political issue of the day was the distribution of the surplus!

convertibility, and in early 1819 the first congressional debate over amending the monetary standard occurred.

In January 1819, Congress adopted the resolution of the representative from South Carolina (Mr. Lowndes) calling for the establishment of a committee to examine the monetary system. The committee, chaired by Lowndes, recommended the adoption of a monetary system similar to that of Britain. The relative mint prices of gold to silver would rise to 15.6, and the gold content of the eagle would fall to 227.98 grains. Silver would be only limited legal tender (in payments up to $5) and a seignorage fee would be charged for coining silver. Lowndes's report stimulated the House of Representatives (in March 1819) to pass a resolution requiring the secretary of the treasury (William Crawford) to present a report on the state of the banking industry and on "such measures as, in his opinion, may be expedient to procure and retain a sufficient quantity of gold and silver coin in the United States, or to supply a circulating medium in place of specie, adapted to the exigencies of the country, and within the power of the government" (Crawford, 1820: 503).

In February 1820 Crawford reported. He suggested (1820: 518) that to "procure and retain" sufficient specie required banking changes: if banks could be restrained from issuing small-denomination notes and from "excessive issues" then fluctuation in the currency could be avoided. He also advocated raising the value of the gold coin by 5 percent to encourage its importation: "this augmentation in its value would cause it to be imported in quantities sufficient to perform all the functions of currency". Following his implicit mandate Crawford also paid considerable attention to the possibility of a fiat paper currency. He noted that "no such paper currency has ever existed" (p. 529) and wrote down the necessary conditions for monetary stability under such a regime before arguing that it would do little to help the economy, especially for the South and West, the regions most clamouring for monetary expansion.

The following year the House directed a subcommittee to examine the "expediency of increasing the relative value of the gold hereafter to be coined at the mint". The subcommittee argued that few U.S. gold coins had been minted, and that those that had, had been exported. The committee argued that while the reason for the ratio of 15 to 1 was not relevant: "It is sufficient to know from unhappy experience, that its tendency is to rid us of a gold currency and leave us nothing but silver" (U.S. Senate, 1879: 556).

The subcommittee considered the possibility of endorsing (whether by act of omission or commission was not discussed) a silver standard, and rejected such a system. The subcommittee argued that the nation needed a more portable medium of exchange in case of war and proceeded to report a bill that raised the value of the gold coins. But the bill was not enacted, and the debate over the ratio and the standard died away.

Late in the 1820s debate resumed when the Senate resolved to ask the secretary of the treasury, now Samuel Ingham, to report on what alteration in the gold coin would be needed to make its relative value conform to that of the silver coinage. In May 1830 Ingham reported.[12] Like

---

[12] In the meantime the Senate had established its own committee, chaired by Sanford, which reported in January 1830.

Crawford, Ingham found this an opportunity to wax elo-
quent on the history of money and the alternative monetary regimes that the nation could adopt. Noting that gold
was not found in general circulation even prior to 1820, he
argued that the scarcity of gold reflected the availability of
bank notes more than the undervaluation of gold. He
further argued that the premium on gold was directly
related to the premium on exchange. That is, as long as the
United States had a balance-of-payments surplus, so that
bills of exchange (on London) were at a premium, there
would be no premium on gold. The gold premium would
be at a maximum when silver had to be exported.

Ingham advocated the adoption of a silver standard.
He argued that bank notes could reasonably replace
gold coins but not the smaller silver coins, since small-
denomination bank notes were turned over so frequently
that they quickly became defaced and worn and therefore
were easily counterfeited. A shortage of gold coins did not
appear to him to be very serious, while a lack of silver coins
would be very injurious to commerce. He opposed "any
measure that introduced into the currency for small
payments any medium which is not itself a standard
measure of property" (Ingham, 1830: 579). That is, he
explicitly rejected the British solution to the problems
of bimetallism, a gold standard with token silver coinage,
that the United States was to accept twenty-three years
later.

Ingham noted that if the weight of coins were reduced
every time a metal became undervalued, the ratchet effect
would work to depreciate the currency over time. Yet his
mandate was to state the change in gold coinage necessary
to bring it into line with the silver coins and the market

ratio, and he concluded by doing so. He wrote favourably of choosing a ratio of 15.5:1, although admitting that that would still undervalue gold, in order to harmonise with the ratio used in France.[13] Ultimately he advocated a ratio of 1:15.625 to 1, because it came close to that in the market (which he estimated at 15.8:1) and could be expressed in definite numbers, as could the standard and pure weight of the eagle (237.6 grs. and 259.2 grs. respectively).

In preparing his report, Ingham solicited advice from Albert Gallatin, an ex-secretary of the treasury (and at that time president of the National Bank of New York City), and John White, Cashier of the Bank of the United States, amongst others, and included their responses as an Appendix to his Report. Gallatin, without making a specific recommendation, opposed the exclusion of silver because he believed it is the "standard of value", it is in greater supply, it requires a greater premium on the exchanges before it can be exported and it is "the only practical remedy against over issues of the worst species of paper currency [small notes]". (Gallatin, 1829: 597)[14]

---

[13] In an early argument for international bimetallism (advocated widely in the 1880s), Ingham argued that an ideal bimetallic standard would be characterized by a common ratio across countries. However, he did not believe that countries were ready to abandon their sovereignty or national ambitions to do this.

[14] He is more virulent than Ingham on the subject of British silver tokens: "Not only has England, by that experiment, in the face of the universal experience of mankind, gratuitously subjected herself to actual inconvenience, for the sake of adhering to an abstract principle; but in so doing, she has departed much more widely from her own principles, and from those which regulate a sound metallic currency. . . . [Token money] is, in fact, an issue of adulterated money;

White argued for the status quo. He argued that unlike many European countries, the United States had a circulation primarily composed of bank notes and whether gold or silver were exported is not very important: "If any evil or real inconvenience has been experienced, I must confess my inability to perceive it" (White, 1830: 659). Using the example of the large gold coinage of Holland when gold coins were not legal tender there, he argued that coinage had less to do with legal tender laws and more to do with the quality of the product.

The Senate meanwhile had passed the resolution of the Senate committee to lower the gold content of the eagle to 254 (38/53) grains and raise the relative value of gold from 15 to 15.625. The House established its own committee to examine the coinage, chaired by C. P. White, a representative from New York, which reported in March 1831 in favour of either a silver standard or a ratio of 15.625. In December 1831 the House established another committee again chaired by White, which again recommended lowering the weight of the eagle, and establishment of a ratio of 15.625.

In May 1832 a motion passed the House calling for the examination of a monetary system in which silver would be legal tender and gold coins would be assayed and minted but would not be legal tender. The government

which does not regulate itself; which, on account of the profit in the coinage, there is a strong temptation to issue beyond what is actually wanted for the object intended; which, being irredeemable, is therefore liable to fluctuation between its nominal and intrinsic value; and which by its connexion with the 20s and 40s gold coins, deranges, or may derange the whole system of British currency".

would accept the coins at rates posted at regular inter-
vals.[15] In 1832 White's committee made two further reports
to the House, again recommending the ratio of 15.625, and
in February 1834 he introduced a bill incorporating this
recommendation. But one week prior to the passage of the
bill in June he altered it to impose a lower weight for the
eagle and a market ratio of 16:1.[16] The bill, reducing the
pure gold content of the Eagle from 247.5 grains to 232
grains, and the standard weight of the coin to 258 grains,
passed both houses.[17]

The ratio of 16:1, while discussed in some Committee
reports, was in every case considered in excess of the
relative market values of gold and silver, and almost
uniformly those who sought an increased value for gold
at the mint recommended a relative value of 15.625:1.
The ultimate choice of a ratio of 16:1 therefore remains
something of a puzzle. Two factors additional to those
mentioned above are sometimes proposed: a desire for
gold coins to remove the need for the Second Bank
(O'Leary, 1937); and a desire to raise the incomes of gold

[15] A similar system had been implemented in France after the suggestion of Mirabeau in 1795, but it was repealed a few years later on the
grounds that no gold coin had been minted and that it therefore
demonetized gold. See Chapter 6.

[16] In 1837, as one of a number of housekeeping measures, the fineness
of both silver and gold coins was made 90% with the standard weight
of the silver coin increasing to 412.5 grains (no change in its fine silver
content) and the weight of the eagle remaining at 258 grains (with
an increase in its fine weight to 232.2 grains). The relative values of
gold to silver therefore changed to 15.988.

[17] This change had an unexpected consequence in that the Supreme
Court subsequently used it as a precedent for the government's con-
stitutional right to devalue the money.

miners and owners in the southern states. We consider them in turn.

The Second Bank of the United States operated as a primitive central bank; it issued notes and kept the government's deposits. It did not act as a lender of last resort, and state-chartered banks could also issue notes, although they did not branch across state lines. One of the functions of the Second Bank was to assist in clearing interregional balances, and it frequently returned notes issued by state banks and demanded that they be redeemed, creating powerful enemies.[18] The Bank's charter was valid for twenty years, and therefore would need renewing in 1836 if the Second Bank were to continue operations. In 1829 Andrew Jackson became President of the United States, and promised to eliminate the Second Bank's monopoly, even if that meant eliminating the Bank, which it did. There is a vast literature on the Bank War, and here our interest is only in the interaction between the Bank War and the coinage legislation.[19] That is, to what extent did advocates of the elimination of the Second Bank believe that an increase in the relative value of gold at the mint would provide a cheap substitute for the Second Bank's interregional clearing facilities?

The answer probably lies in two parts. Why was there a move to change the relative value of coins at the mint, and why was the ratio of 16:1 adopted? The latter may well

---

[18] Remini (1967) summarizes the groups opposed and supporting the Bank, and suggests that while the bank had incurred widespread enmity, a majority of Americans may have favored the recharter of the bank.

[19] Temin (1975), Remini (1967), and Hammond (1957) provide a survey of analyses and references.

have been a fallout of the Bank War. The legislation introduced by C. P. White, a New York Jacksonian, reflected bills
that had been prepared by committee and discussions that
had been in process for several years. But the bill recommended a reduction of the weight of the eagle so that the
ratio was 15.625:1 rather than 16:1. The change to 16:1
occurred at the last minute, and history is unclear why the
bill passed so easily with bipartisan support.

The desire to raise the value of gold, however, preceded
the rise of the Jacksonians and reflected persistent concerns about the monetary system. While the history of the
period emphasizes the interaction between coinage legislation and bank notes – specifically small-denomination
notes – raising the value of gold at the mint would do
nothing to decrease such issues, and might (as in fact it
did in the late 1840s) increase the problem.

The last factor to be considered is the interest of the
gold mining areas of the South. From 1825, growing
volumes of gold were extracted from the mines primarily
of North Carolina and Georgia. From 1830 to 1833, of the
$784,000 gold coin minted annually, $633,000 came from
mines in the southern United States.[20] It was widely argued
that the substitution of gold for silver as the national
medium of exchange would imply a large increase in
demand for gold and a dramatic benefit for the mine inter-
ests. In practice, the demand for gold was elastic, and the
benefit was marginal. The official price of gold at the mint
rose by 6.7%, and would have risen by 4.2% if the ratio
had risen to 15.625:1. However, as noted above, gold

[20] In contrast, the California gold rush produced about $150 million per
year from 1850 to 1855.

traded at a premium and so the incremental benefit was less.

COINING TECHNOLOGY

The early post-Revolutionary period had seen almost as much debate over the need for a mint as over the question of the standard. The alternative, which had received considerable support, was the use of "contracted" coinage, and Taxay (1966) describes the considerable correspondence between U.S. officials and Boulton over contracts for a copper coinage in particular. However, Congress voted in favour of a domestic coinage and established the mint in 1792. The mint was designed to employ steam engines, in order that the coining presses would be sufficiently powerful to stamp the dollar coin, but while "waiting" for the steam engines, horses were used to power the rolling mill and humans powered the three coining presses.[21]

The mint was inefficient and consequently underemployed. As late as 1802 Congress discussed a bill to abolish the mint, use imported gold and silver coins and contract out the copper coinage. In 1799, and again in 1801, Mint officials wrote letters to Mathew Boulton asking him to

---

[21] Taxay (1966: 82) cites a letter from the chief coiner Henry Voigt to the director (Boudinot) explaining the lack of steam engines: "it was no error of the director [then Rittenhouse] that horses were employed, they only were protemporary till it should be found more convenient to erect a steam engine; for he knew perfectly well, that horses were insufficient to make Dollars to advantage".

225

quote prices for "a compleat Apparatus of a Mint on your own best approved plan, with a steam Engine equal to the force of 8 Horses".[22] In 1816 the mint burned down, and the new mint did purchase a 10 horsepower steam engine to drive the rolling presses and planchet cutter, but the coining presses continued to be human powered.

In 1828 the House committee on the mint recommended rebuilding the mint, and including "the new combination of machinery devised and executed by Mr. Boulton" (Taxay, 1966: 144). In 1829 Congress approved funding for the changes, but when the new mint building was occupied in January 1833, the machinery was simply transferred from the old building. Two years later the director of the mint sent Franklin Peale to Europe for two years to study the technological innovations in place there. He returned with improved methods of assaying silver and plans for new milling machines and coining presses which would be driven by steam (Taxay, 1966: 166). In arguing to the secretary of the treasury for the merits of the new presses, Director Robert Patterson said, "one of the most important [advantages] is that [it] admits the immediate and easy application of steam power. At present our larger presses require the operation of three men each, while I am sure that one man could attend two of the new presses. The work too may be done much more rapidly". In 1836 the new coining press, which copied the knee joint method of Uhlhorn and Thonnelier rather than the lever press of Boulton, was operational.

[22] Director Boudinot to Boulton, 6 November 1799, cited in Taxay (1966: 133; see also p. 135).

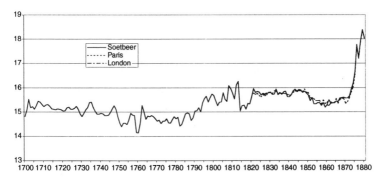

Figure 7.1. Estimates of the gold/silver ratio. Sources: Laughlin (1892: 221–3); Flandreau (1995: 340–1).

THE PERFORMANCE OF BIMETALLISM, 1792–1853

Figure 7.1 illustrates Soetbeer's (1879) data on the relative price of gold to silver from 1700 to 1878 and Flandreau's (1995) data on the ratio in Paris and London. Soetbeer's data are based on twice weekly market prices for gold and silver in Hamburg, and are accepted as the most accurate – for that city at least. Flandreau's data are drawn from the Paris mint, while the London data are based on the price of silver in the London market. The figure shows that the ratio of 15:1 chosen by Hamilton was almost exactly the relative price of gold in Europe at that time, and that gold appreciated in relative terms immediately thereafter. The price behaved in a somewhat erratic manner during the War of 1812, but between 1821 and 1833 remained close to 15.75, at which rate the mint ratio of 15:1 undervalued gold by 5%.

The mint ratio of 16:1 introduced in 1834 however, overvalued gold. The degree of overvaluation was slight in the 1830s and 1840s but became significant in the 1850s when the California gold rush increased the stock of gold sufficiently to reduce the relative price of gold to silver from 15.85 in 1848 to 15.19 in 1859. After 1859 the price of gold gradually rose until 1872, and then, as we have seen in Chapter 5, dramatically increased.

Our knowledge of the specie market in the United States is still fragmentary. New York newspapers provide semiweekly price quotations for a variety of gold and silver coins in New York, Philadelphia, Boston and Baltimore. Figure 7.2 shows the premia on Spanish dollars, and American gold (after 1834, old, i.e., heavy, eagles).[23] It is not clear whether these prices reflect market transactions or standing offers to buy at a bank. The volatility of the prices gives us some confidence that they are close to market prices. We assume that the numeraire is implicitly American silver dollars before 1834 (for which no prices are given prior to 1834), and new American gold coins after 1834 and that payments were typically effected in convertible bank notes.[24] From the mid-1820s there was a small premium on American gold, and a very small premium on Spanish silver.

The effect of the legislation in 1834 is clear in the data.

---

[23] Prices are from the first observation of each month, and are taken from the *New York shipping and commercial* list for 1816–33, and from the *New York Advertiser* from 1833–48. The overlap between the two sources suggests that these are the same series.

[24] From May 1837 to May 1838, the numeraire would have been inconvertible bank notes, explaining the high prices for Spanish dollars and American gold during those months.

228

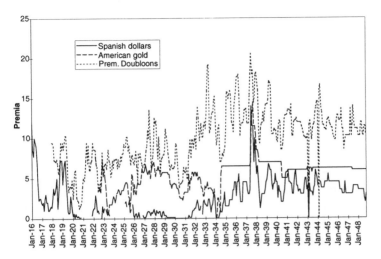

Figure 7.2. U.S. coin prices. Source: See text.

If coins traded at a premium reflecting their intrinsic value, with the overvalued coin being the numeraire, the old eagles should have traded at a constant 6.7% premium (the old eagle had 6.7% more gold than the new eagle) and silver coins should have traded at variable premium between 0% and 5%. The data show that indeed the old eagles rose to a premium that (with the exception of during the 1837–38 financial crisis) was virtually constant, at a rate between 5% and 7%. The silver coins were traded at varying premia between 1% and 6%. The very high premia in 1837 reflected the suspension of bank note convertibility by New York (and other) banks in 1837–38, and the fact that the quotations are the prices of coins in bank notes.

The amount of gold and silver coin minted in the United

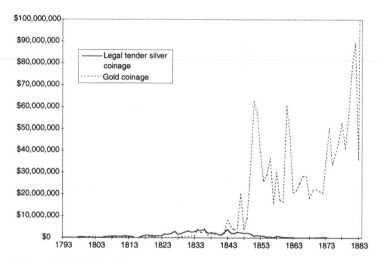

Figure 7.3. U.S. coinage of gold and silver. Source: Laughlin
(1892: 249–50).

States is shown in Figure 7.3.[25] In the period up to 1814
both gold and silver were coined with gold dominating in
some periods, silver in others. After 1817 (and with the
exception of 1820) the majority of the coinage before 1834
was silver. Figure 7.4 shows more starkly the relationship
between coinage and overvaluation. With the exception of
the period 1814–20, the more that silver is overvalued at
the mint, the greater is the share of silver coined at the
mint.

[25] Data are from Laughlin (1896). The data on legal tender coinage
from 1853–73 were estimated assuming that 9.6% of the annual
coinage was legal tender, and the rest was on government account.
The proportion 9.6% is adopted because over the entire period,
90.4% of the silver coinage was on government account (U.S. Senate,
1879: 103).

230

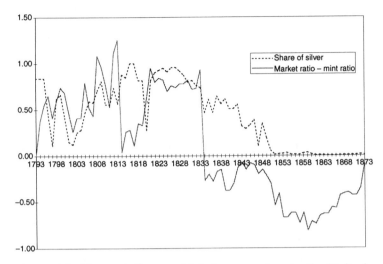

Figure 7.4. Share of silver and Market premium in the United States, 1793–1834.

Whether or not such an amount of coinage would have significantly affected the share of gold and silver in the stock of circulating medium is of course difficult to tell. Data on the stock of specie in any particular year are suspect, as are the data on trade flows. In 1820 the secretary of the treasury estimated that the stock of specie and bullion in the United States in 1820 was $20 million, of which $4.5 million was in circulation and the remainder in bank vaults (U.S. Senate, 1879: 504). It is reported that $89.5 million was imported and $88.6 million exported over the ensuing 14 years.[26] During the period 1821–33, the mint produced $29.7 million in coins – $25.3 million in silver, and $4.4 million in gold. Large amounts of imported bullion and perhaps coin never went to the mint.

[26] Data are from *Hunt's Merchants' Magazine* (1842), Vol. 7, p. 568.

231

Between 1834 and 1850 the U.S. mint overvalued gold; however, the extent of undervaluation was small and silver coins continued to be minted and, by all reports, to circulate. The domestic silver coin was supplemented by Spanish silver coins (bits and 2 bits) which circulated at traditional values (of 12.5c and 25c, respectively) in excess of their intrinsic value. The gold discoveries in the late 1840s and increased gold production in the 1850s created a dramatic change in the currency. The price of silver (relative to gold) rose and even the worn coin and Spanish silver coins were withdrawn from the circulation. The experience, described in detail by Martin (1973), provides clear support for the modified version of Gresham's Law: the low-denomination coin did not circulate at a premium but was withdrawn from circulation. After 1850 very little (full legal tender) silver was coined at the U.S. mint; however, after 1853 subsidiary coins with limited legal tender were minted on government account. We turn now to those issues.

THE INTRODUCTION OF TOKEN SILVER AND THE "CRIME" OF 1873

The U.S. legislative response to the fall in the price of gold in 1850 was similar to that of France ten years later, although as at the beginning of the Republic there was much less debate over the issue in the United States. In December 1851 the secretary of the treasury recommended reducing all silver coins to "token" by reducing their weight by 7.7%. Since silver was then undervalued by about 5%, this would overvalue silver; however, he recommended that silver coins be limited legal tender and only be minted on government account. The chairman of the Senate Finance Committee (Hunter) introduced a bill incorporating some of these provisions but which called for only a 6.9% decrease in the weight of the coins and limited their legal tender to $5. Hunter argued that the bill was not intended to end bimetallism and specifically omitted the dollar coin from the weight reduction.[27]

Although the House Ways and Means Committee argued for elimination of all legal tender status for the subsidiary coins, the bill Hunter had proposed was passed in February 1853. The law stated that the amount of subsidiary coinage was to be determined by the Treasury and the mint was to purchase silver bullion (with gold) and to pay out subsidiary silver to all who demanded it. The legislation did not make any provision for convertibility of the coins, with the result that by the mid-1850s there were complaints of excessive amounts of the coins (Taxay, 1966: 226). The onset of the Civil War, and consequent issue of legal tender "greenbacks", removed the urgency of this problem. The greenbacks drove gold coin to a premium, and even the "token" silver coins contained silver worth more (in paper money) than their face value. In 1879 legislation was passed requiring the Treasury to redeem silver coins (of less than $1 in face value).

---

[27] Although the Act of 1873, discussed below, terminated the right to mint silver dollars, many economists – certainly from Laughlin (1896: 92) on – argued that with the legislation of February 1853 "it had been agreed to accept the situation by which we had come to have gold for large payments, and to relegate silver to a limited service in the subsidiary coins".

As in the example of France, the interesting characteristic of the introduction of token silver coins into the United States lies in the roads not taken. The traditional bimetallic response would have been to decrease the weight of the silver coinage.[28] Alternatively, the silver or gold coins could have been minted without an explicit legal tender value. Martin (1973) notes that these alternatives were all discussed by contemporaries but none were adopted. The United States chose the practical course of a de facto gold standard without the need to legislate it.

The traditional response had been chosen twenty years earlier, when silver was the dominant metal for domestic coin. Laughlin (1896: 80) argues, as does Gallarotti (1990), that the asymmetry reflected an inherent prejudice in favour of gold. But in the United States, as elsewhere, the use of token silver coins eliminated the medium of exchange basis for bimetallism; only later were other rationales for bimetallism to dominate.

By 1873, the United States was on a de facto gold standard, and the need for bimetallism either to provide small-denomination coins or to increase the money stock had been eliminated by the issue of token subsidiary coins and a variety of paper money. As in France and England in similar circumstances, the United States acted to abandon bimetallism, and the Coinage Act of 1873 ended the free

---

[28] The traditional response was to increase the mint equivalent of the undervalued metal, here silver. This could have been done by reducing the weight of the coins or by increasing their value. Since the value of silver coins lay in their aliquot nature, the former was the adjustment of choice.

coinage of (unlimited) legal tender silver coins. But in the United States, the story did not end here, and for the next twenty-five years a return to bimetallism was proposed, debated and, at least according to the Sherman Act, partially adopted.[29]

The facts concerning the U.S. murky adherence to the gold standard between 1873 and 1900 are well known.[30] In 1873 after three years of debate the U.S. Congress passed the Coinage Act of 1873, which essentially "cleaned up" legislation concerning the coinage over the previous eighty years. The law detailed every aspect of coinage and in Section 15 listed the silver coins of the United States as: half-dollar, quarter-dollar and dime; plus a trade dollar weighing 420 grains (90% fine). Each coin was to be legal tender up to $5.[31] The subsidiary coins were to be coined only on government account, as they had been since 1853, and the trade dollar would be freely, but not gratuitously,

---

[29] In Britain and France there were also discussions of the return to bimetallism, but the proposal never met with the success of the bimetallists in the United States. It is difficult to assign probabilities for the return to bimetallism after 1873, but Garber's use of option pricing to analyze bimetallic bonds suggests a possible methodology. For a series of nineteenth-century U.S. bonds, Garber estimates the price that the bond would trade at (1) if it were a commitment to pay the face value in gold, and (2) if it were a commitment allowing the debtor to choose whether to pay in gold or silver. Comparing the actual price of bonds issued in 1878 with the predicted gold bond price and predicted bimetallic bond price suggests that agents priced them as though they were gold bonds.

[30] The seminal account is that of Friedman and Schwartz (1963).

[31] The (limited) legal tender status of the trade dollar was removed in 1876.

coined. The critical omission in the legislation was the omission of the free coinage of the unlimited legal tender traditional silver dollar.

Since virtually no silver coinage other than the subsidiary coinage on government account had occurred for at least twenty years, and the silver dollar had not been coined since 1836, the impact of the legislation may not have been immediately obvious.[32] However, in 1875 the passage of the Resumption Act requiring the government to make greenbacks convertible at par by 1 January 1879 made it clear that deflation was imminent. Then, the rapid fall in the price of silver in 1876 meant that if the mint were to buy silver at 1837 prices it would raise the price of silver, and also the general price level. Unsurprisingly a coalition of silver producers and Western debtors emerged in favour of bimetallism.[33]

The coalition never eliminated the gold standard, but it succeeded in requiring the mint to purchase silver and to issue traditional silver dollars with unlimited legal tender. The Coinage Act of 1878 required the mint to issue between $2 and $4 million per month in silver coins, which could be exchanged for silver certificates which were receivable for taxes and which were mainly used for that purpose. In addition, the Act instructed the president to convene an international monetary conference to adopt a common ratio for an international bimetallic standard. The President vetoed the bill, but it became law after passing

[32] Whether or not the legislation was "surreptitious" is one of the many issues in the historical debate over the Crime of 1873. See Friedman (1990) and Laughlin (1896).

[33] Frieden (e.g., 1993) has argued that the concern of the pro-silver forces was with devaluation rather than domestic price inflation.

by more than the two-thirds majority required in both Houses. Since the Treasury redeemed its debts in gold to assuage largely foreign bondholders, and it received taxes in silver or its equivalent, the Treasury subsidy on silver sales was explicit.

In 1890 the Sherman Act repealed the 1878 legislation and required the Treasury to purchase (but, until 1898, not necessarily coin) up to 4.5 million ounces of silver per month. These purchases were to be at the market price, eliminating the loss to the Treasury. The Sherman Act included the rather amazing rationalization: "it being the established policy of the United States to maintain the two metals on a parity with each other upon the present legal ratio". This at a time when the market price of silver was approximately 25% lower than the U.S. mint price!

The showdown between the bimetallists and the gold standard forces came in the famous election of 1896. The bimetallists were represented by the Democratic candidate for the presidency, William Jennings Bryan, who campaigned against the "Cross of Gold".[34] Bryan's electoral defeat, coupled with the gold discoveries of the late 1890s and subsequent economic and price surge, ended the appeal of bimetallism. The gold standard act of 1900 affirmed the gold definition of the dollar, and repealed the Sherman Act purchase clauses. Although it specifically permitted the continued pursuit of international bimetallism, the fire had gone out of that cause. Bryan ran again on the bimetallist platform in 1900 and was again defeated,

---

[34] The most diverting discussion of the monetary battle in the last quarter of the nineteenth century is "The Wizard of Oz", an allegory most recently interpreted by Rockoff (1990).

this time overwhelmingly. In the twentieth century inflation would be advocated through fiat money rather than
modified bimetallism.

HISTORICAL ACCIDENT?

The monetary regimes of the nineteenth-century United
States were perhaps as unstable as in the twentieth
century. Bimetallism established in 1792 was challenged
in the 1820s before being confirmed in 1834; then in 1853
similar challenges led to an implicit rejection of bimetallism, which became explicit in 1873. After 1873, belated
attempts to restore bimetallism left the gold standard's
hold ambiguous until 1900.

Were these regime shifts random wanderings driven by
political struggles, or were there also fundamental monetary forces underlying the changes? The initial choice of
a bimetallic standard came after limited debate and may
have reflected the universal use of bimetallism in Western
economies with which the United States traded. The
undervaluation of gold in the first half of the nineteenth
century led to debate about the appropriate standard:
debate that included concerns about the need for gold coin
as a high-value (low transport cost) means of payment, and
the need for silver coin as a low-value means of payment
(in preference to low-denomination bank notes). The
devaluation of gold in 1834, although the traditional
method of dealing with undervaluation, was not a fore-
gone conclusion.

The response to the undervaluation of silver in the

1850s, a specific rejection of the traditional response, was not a historical accident. The technological improvements to the mint made possible an alternative to low-denomination bank notes other than full-value silver coin, and this alternative was implemented. The fall in the price of silver in the mid-1870s would have led gold to be undervalued at the mint if the Act of 1873 had not intervened. The response of the bimetallists to this introduced new arguments over monetary standards, arguments that challenged the nominal anchor that the West had adopted and which presaged the debates and monetary policies of the twentieth century.

8

Conclusions

Conclusions

The central issue of this book has been the ability of commodity money standards to provide a "nominal anchor". Typical explanations of commodity money standards argue that under a commodity money standard "the price level is determined by the technological conditions relating to production (perhaps abroad) of the commodity in conjunction with the factors governing its demand (these including but not limited to the desire to hold certain quantities of the medium of exchange)" (McCallum, 1989: 23). Thus implicitly the price level is anchored by the "real" economy. The commodity money standard is then contrasted with a fiat money standard in which the monetary authority can determine the price level.

I argue that this is misleading in a nontrivial way.[1] The fact that prices and contracts were stated in a unit of account rather than in (for example) ounces of silver, meant that the price level was "anchored" in part by the conditions listed above, but equally by the relationship that the monetary authorities established between an ounce of silver and the unit of account. The book has focussed on how that relationship was established: what determined the unit of account value of an ounce of gold or silver and why did it change?

We have seen that a variety of forces were involved. Some were outside the State's control: over decades in circulation, coins gradually wore down with use so that a coin of a given face value contained less silver or gold. With the same effect, although not so gradually, clippers and other

---

[1] This is not meant to disparage McCallum's book, which as an undergraduate text puts the case starkly, I think, to make a point and is consistent with virtually all treatments of commodity money.

coin alterers would seek personal gain by removing some of the weight of the coin. As noted in Chapter 3, this became less of a problem after the sixteenth century, with the introduction of milled coins.

More interesting are the factors that influenced the State or monetary authority to change the value of the unit of account, particularly to depreciate the currency by increasing the unit of account value of an ounce of gold or silver. The relevant factors can be loosely placed in three groups: fiscal pressures, monetary pressures and political pressures. The former were particularly prominent in the medieval period, when alternative revenue sources for kings were rarer. Debasement especially by producing greater profits per coin minted, at least temporarily, could provide a large sum relatively quickly and could be used to finance wars, as well as ongoing expenses of a Kingdom. But this seignorage tax was politically expensive and by the mideighteenth century, the English and French avoided depreciating the currency except in periods of war.

Monetary pressures to depreciate the coinage came primarily from the operation of the bimetallic standard. The adoption of a bimetallic standard in which gold and silver coins were given fixed values in the unit of account provided a medium of exchange with large- and small-denomination coins at a legally fixed exchange rate. But it meant that fluctuations in the relative market prices of gold and silver would tend to cause one type of coin to circulate at a premium over par which the monetary authorities would then eliminate by a depreciation. This was particularly common as the value of gold rose in the late sixteenth and seventeenth centuries. While this practice

244

was accepted with little debate then, by the late eighteenth and nineteenth centuries this rationale for depreciating the currency was contentious, as evidenced by the controversy occasioned by Calonne's increase in the value of French gold coins in 1785 and the U.S. reduction in the weight of the gold eagle in 1834.

Finally, political pressure coming from specific interest groups was also a factor in depreciations. Here the arguments ranged from exporters wanting to see a depreciation of the currency, debtors objecting to an (unanticipated) deflation and miners of gold and silver (and copper) who advocated their commodity as a monetary commodity.

By the late nineteenth century the destabilizing forces of bimetallism and fiscal expedience had been reduced: bimetallism had been replaced by a monometallic gold standard and although governments (such as the United States during the Civil War and England during the Napoleonic Wars) used depreciation to finance wars, they returned to the prewar parity after the war. However, there was another noteworthy change in the operation of monetary standards: the transition from a monetary standard in which coins were the primary medium of exchange to one where bank notes – claims on coins – played a more important role. Bank notes were often first issued by private organizations but by the end of the nineteenth century, bank notes in England, France and the United States were a monopoly of the State (or its agency), giving the monetary authorities in those countries an additional mechanism for depreciating the currency. Instead of changing the unit of account value of the coins, the central bank could suspend the convertibility of notes into coins and then force more notes into circulation. For example, the suspension of convertibility by the Bank of England during the Napoleonic Wars and the issue of inconvertible greenbacks during the Civil War.

Yet this new mechanism did not lead to a rash of depreciations. The monetary regime from 1880 to 1914 has been called the classical gold standard, suggesting that it defines, or represents the zenith of, the operation of a commodity money regime, and in a certain respect it did. The stability that had eluded early modern monetary authorities, in large part because of the physical constraints of coins and the fiscal and political constraints on monetary authorities, appeared to be feasible. Why then did the gold standard fall apart in the early twentieth century, never to be restored?

The gold standard carried the seeds of its own destruction. As we have seen, the stability of the gold standard relied on the ability of monetary authorities to issue fiduciary monies – notes and coins convertible on demand into gold. The advantage of fiduciary money over fiat money is that it provides a nominal anchor; the disadvantages are that it generates less seignorage revenue and that the economy is anchored to a rather random spot since the price level depends on such things as the industrial demand for gold and the geological forces affecting the supply of gold. Fiat money offers the possibility of greater seignorage and less dependence on exogenous forces of nature.

Through the nineteenth and early twentieth centuries, monetary authorities reduced the gold reserves behind their monetary liabilities in order to maximize seignorage

Conclusions

and to attempt to deal with what was perceived as a global gold shortage. But, as the reserves ratio fell, the monetary system relied more and more on the credibility of the monetary authority, reducing the advantage of fiduciary money relative to fiat money.

Firstly, the gold exchange standard encouraged many smaller countries to hold reserves not in gold but in notes and deposits of countries like Britain and the United States, whose notes were convertible into gold. Then, under the Bretton Woods agreement, signatories agreed to make their currency convertible into U.S. dollars, and only U.S. dollars would be convertible directly into gold. These steps increased the vulnerability of the system.

The gold standard collapsed like a bad actor – staggering around the world stage for sixty years until its final demise in the early 1970s. Two events were pivotal: the abandonment of the gold standard in the 1930s and the breakdown of the Bretton Woods system in the 1970s. In 1931 Britain suspended the convertibility of Bank of England notes into gold, and in 1933 and 1936 respectively the United States and France took similar actions. The remarkable characteristic of these actions was the absence of a wartime threat, or motivation for the suspension. Instead the action was motivated by the problems inherent in a fractional reserve monetary system. All three central banks issued notes that were only partially backed by gold yet were redeemable in gold on demand. Fractional reserve backing is profitable for the note issuer (here central bank) but if all noteholders want to redeem their notes they will not be able to. Such a bank "run" will necessarily trigger a suspension of convertibility.

In the twentieth century, central banks attempted to maintain the advantage of the gold standard – that a fixed definition of the unit of account provided a clear nominal anchor – while also having the advantage of resource savings by using a fractional reserve system. This system reached its epitome under the Bretton Woods system whereby central banks would maintain convertibility into U.S. dollars, which alone would be convertible on demand into gold. The system foundered when the United States wanted to expand its monetary supply, in part to finance the Vietnam War, ushering in a brief era of floating exchange rates.

With the suspension of the Bretton Woods system, monetary authorities used monetary policy to address domestic problems, typically to mitigate business cycle problems, and in part to address problems arising from the volatility of oil prices. Internationally, floating exchange rates reigned. Yet the heyday of nationalistic monetary policies and truly floating exchange rates was short-lived and at the end of the twentieth century monetary authorities are again tying their own hands. Two types of institutional responses suggest the perceived importance of currency stability: currency unions and currency boards. The adoption of a common currency by many Western European nations reflects a desire to return to nineteenth-century stability, and a willingness to forgo the use of monetary policy as an instrument for domestic goals in exchange for a stable and unitary exchange rate. Currency boards – whereby a currency such as the Argentine peso is 100% backed by a hard currency such as the U.S. dollar – reflect a similar desire for exchange rate stability. Currency boards imply that a country gives up the potential savings from issuing an unbacked monetary base in order to make it clear that the monetary authorities will not attempt to exploit the monetary system for fiscal reasons.

Neither institution – currency union or currency board – returns us to the nineteenth century. The European nations have delegated the monetary policy of their entity to the European central bank, but the mandate of the bank is unclear, as is its ability to carry out that mandate. Currency boards tie one currency to another, but the pair is not anchored to anything. Theorists have suggested a variety of nominal anchors – inflation targets, nominal GDP targets, exchange rate targets – but no consensus has been reached amongst either monetary economists or monetary authorities.

References

PRINCIPAL ARCHIVAL SOURCES

Bank of England

Court Directors Books, 1809–36
Committee of Treasury Reports, 1140/4, 1140/5
Committee of Treasury Minutes, 1816–35

Public Records Office

Committee on Coin – Minutes and Papers: BT6 117–29.
Treasury Papers: T1 – misc records
Royal Mint: Mint Record Books, 1-18–1-28;
              Misc. mint records 1-54, 2-17; 2-14.

Paris Mint

Series E: Technologie
Series K: Questions monétaires
Series L: Rapports avec les ministres
Registre: Commission de la monnaie (194, 195, 217, 202).

251

References

REFERENCES CITED

Academie des Sciences Morales et politiques. 1902. *Ordonnances des Rois de France*, Paris: Imprimerie Nationale, 7 vols. (Cited as *Ordonnances*.)

Allen, R. C. 1998. Historical Price Indexes. Unpublished manuscript.

Babut, A. 1907. *Deux documents relatifs à l'installation de la machine à vapeur Périer à la monnaie de Paris en l'an IV*. Paris.

Banque de France. 1841. Compte Rendu Pour l'Exercice 1841. *Journal des économistes*, 1: 322–4.

Barro, R., and D. Gordon. 1983. Rules, Discretion and Reputation in a Model of Monetary Policy. *Journal of Monetary Economics*, 12: 101–21.

Baudrillard, H. 1865. Des crises monétaires et le question de l'or. *Journal des économistes*, 7: 360–89.

Bérenger. 1802. Premier Rapport sur le projet de loi relatif aux monnaies. Paris. Reprinted in M. Chevalier, *De la baisse probable*, Paris, 1859, pp. 156–63.

Bisson, Thomas N. 1979. *Conservation of Coinage*. Clarendon: Oxford University Press.

Blanchet, A., and A. Dieudonné. 1916. *Manuel de Numismatique Française*. Paris: Auguste Picard.

Bloch, M. 1954. *Esquisse d'une histoire monetaire de l'Europe*. Paris: Cahiers des Annales.

Bodin, Jean. 1606. *The Six Bookes of a Commonweale*. Reprinted 1962, Cambridge, Mass.: Harvard University Press.

Boizard, J. 1696. *Traite des monnaies*. Paris.

Bordo, M., and F. Kydland. 1995. The Gold Standard as a Rule: An Essay in Exploration. *Explorations in Economic History*, 32: 423–65.

References

Bordo, M., and H. Rockoff. 1996. The Gold Standard as a "Good Housekeeping Seal of Approval." *Journal of Economic History* (June): 389–428.

Boyne, W. 1889–91. *Trade Tokens Issued in the Seventeenth Century*. Ed. G. C. Williamson. London: E. Stock.

Breckinridge, S. P. 1903. *Legal Tender*. Chicago: University of Chicago Press.

Brooke, G. C. 1932. *English Coins*, London: Methuen.

Brown, H. P., and S. V. Hopkins. 1981. *A Perspective of Wages and Prices*. London: Methuen.

Carothers, N. 1930. *Fractional Money*. New York.

Carson, R. A. G. 1962. *Coins of the World*. New York: Harper.

Cernuschi, H. 1876. *M. Michel Chevalier et le bimétallisme*. Paris. 1887. *The Bimetallic Par*. London: P. S. King.

Challis, C. E. 1978. *The Tudor Coinage*. Manchester: The University Press.

    ed. 1992. *A New History of the Royal Mint*. Cambridge: Cambridge University Press.

Chausserie-Laprée, P. 1911. *L'Union monétaire latine*. Paris: Arthur Rousseau.

Chevalier, M. 1859. *De la baisse probable de l'or*. Paris: Capelle.

Cipolla, C. 1956. *Money, Prices and Civilization in the Mediterranean World*. Princeton, N.J.: Princeton University Press.

    1983. *The Monetary Policy of Fourteenth-Century Florence*. Berkeley: University of California Press.

Cooper, R. 1987. *The International Monetary System*. Cambridge, Mass.: Harvard University Press.

Coquelin, C. 1844. Des monnaies en France, et d'une réforme du système monétaire français. *Revue des deux mondes*, 15 (October).

    1851. De la dépréciation de l'or et du système monétaire français. *Journal des économistes*, 117: 55–67.

References

Costes, H. 1885. *Les institutions monétaires de la France*. Paris: Guillaumin.

Craig, John. 1953. *The Mint*. Cambridge: Cambridge University Press.

Cramer, J. A. 1741. *Elements of the Art of Assaying*. London.

Crawford, W. 1820. Report on Currency to the House of Representatives. Reprinted 1979 in U.S. Senate, *International Monetary Conference*, Senate Exec. Doc. No. 58, 45th Congress, 3rd Session. Arno Press, pp. 502–41.

Cretet. 1798. Rapport sur la loi des monnaies, fait au conseil des anciens. Paris. Reprinted in M. Chevalier (1859), pp. 91–105.

Darnis, J-M. 1988. *La monnaie de Paris*. Paris.

Del Mar, A. 1867. *Money and Civilization*. Republished New York, 1969.

Deitz, F. C. 1923. The Exchequer in Elizabeth's Reign. *Smith College Studies in History*, 8.

Despaux, A. 1936. *Les dévaluations monétaires dans l'histoire*. Paris: Marcel Riviere.

Dickinson, H. W. 1937. *Mathew Boulton*. Cambridge: Cambridge University Press.

Doty, R. G. 1993. The Industrialisation of Money: Three Examples. In M. M. Archibald and M. R. Cowell, eds., *Metallurgy in Numismatics*, Vol. 3. London: Royal Numismatic Society, Special Publication No. 24.

Dumas, E. 1856. *Essai sur la fabrication des monnaies*. Ms. 8^0-762. Rouen.

1868. *Notes sur l'émission en France des monnaies décimales de bronze, 1852–65*. Ms. 4^0-464.

Einaudi, L. 1953. The Theory of Imaginary Money from Charlemagne to the French Revolution. In Frederic Lane and Jelke C. Riemersma, eds., *Enterprise and Secular Change*. London, pp. 228–61.

References

Ercker, L. 1696. *Fleta Minor: Assays of Lazarus Erckern.* Tr. John Pettus. London: S. Bateman.

Feaveryear, A. 1963. *The Pound Sterling.* Oxford: Clarendon Press.

Ferguson, E. James. 1961. *The Power of the Purse.* Chapel Hill: University of North Carolina Press.

Fetter, Frank W. 1931. Some Neglected Aspects of Gresham's Law. *Quarterly Journal of Economics*: 480–495.

1965. *The Development of British Monetary Orthodoxy.* Cambridge, Mass.: Harvard University Press.

Fetter, Frank W., and D. Gregory. 1973. *Monetary and Financial Policy.* Dublin: Irish University Press.

Fisher, I. 1913. *The Purchasing Power of Money.* New York.

Flandreau, M. 1995. *L'or du monde.* Paris: L'Harmattan.

Flandreau, M. 1996. The French Crime of 1873: An Essay on the Emergence of the International Gold Standard, 1870–1880. *Journal of Economic History* (December): 862–97.

n.d. As Good as Gold? Bimetallism in Equilibrium, 1848–1873. Unpublished manuscript. University of California at Berkeley.

Fould, A. 1866. "The Origin of the Monetary Union Called 'Latin', 1865." Reprinted in United States Senate (1879 [1978]), pp. 781–6.

Frieden, J. 1993. The Dynamics of International Monetary Systems: International and Domestic Factors in the Rise, Reign, and Demise of the Classical Gold Standard. In J. Snyder and R. Jervis, eds., *Coping with Complexity in the International System.* Boulder, Colo.: Westview Press, pp. 137–62.

Friedman, M. 1990. Bimetallism Revisited. *Journal of Economic Perspectives*, 4: 85–104.

Friedman, M., and A. Schwartz. 1963. *A Monetary History of the*

References

United States, 1867–1960. Princeton, N.J.: Princeton University Press.

Gadoury, V., and F. Droulers. 1978. *Les monnaies royales français de Louis XIII à Louis XVI 1610–1792.* Monte Carlo: Gadoury.

Galbraith, John K. 1975. *Money: Whence It Came, Where It Went.* Boston: Houghton Mifflin.

Gallarotti, G. 1993. The Scramble for Gold: Monetary Regime Transformation in the 1870s. In M. D. Bordo and F. Capie, eds., *Monetary Regimes in Transition.* Cambridge: Cambridge University Press, pp. 15–67.

Gallatin, A. P. 1829. Letter to Hon. S. D. Ingham, on the Relative Value of Gold and Silver. Reprinted 1979 in U.S. Senate, *International Monetary Conference*, Senate Exec. Doc. No. 58, 45th Congress, 3rd Session. Arno Press, pp. 589–97.

Garber, P. 1986. Nominal Contracts in a Bimetallic Standard. *American Economic Review.* December: 1012–30.

Gaudin. 1801. "Premier Rapport" and Second Rapport aux Consuls de la République. Paris. Reprinted in M. Chevalier, *De la baisse probable*, pp. 106–55; 188–98.

Giovannini, A. 1993. Bretton Woods and Its Precursors: Rules versus Discretion in the History of International Monetary Regimes. In M. Bordo and B. Eichengreen, eds., *A Retrospective on the Bretton Woods System.* Chicago: University of Chicago Press, pp. 109–54.

Glassman, D., and A. Redish. 1988. Currency Depreciation in Early Modern England and France. *Explorations in Economic History,* 25: 75–97.

Gould, J. D. 1970. *The Great Debasement.* Oxford: Clarendon Press.

Great Britain, Parliamentary Papers. Report of the International Conference on Weights, Measures and Coin. British Parliament Papers, 1867–8 [4021] XXVII.801.

256

References

Greenfield, R., and H. Rockoff. 1995. Gresham's Law in Nineteenth Century America. *Journal of Money, Credit and Banking*, 24: 1086–98.

Hamilton, A. 1791. Report on the Establishment of a Mint. Reprinted in H. Syrett, ed., *The Papers of Alexander Hamilton*, Vol. VII, pp. 570–607. New York Columbia University Press, 1962.

Hammond, B. 1957. *Banking and Politics in America*. Princeton, N.J.: Princeton University Press.

Harris, J. 1757. *An Essay upon Money and Coins*. London: Reprinted in McCullough (1856), 1966: 339–512.

Harsin, Paul. 1928. *Les doctrines monétaires et financières en France*. Paris: Librairie Félix Alcan.

Hawtrey, R. 1923. *Currency and Credit*. London: Longmans, Green and Co.

Hepburn, A. B. 1915. *A History of Currency in the United States*. New York: Macmillan.

Hocking. 1909. Simon's Dies in the Royal Mint Museum with Some Notes on the Early History of Coinage by Machine. *Numismatic Chronicle*, ser. 4 vol. 9.

Ingham, S. D. 1830. Report Respecting the Relative Value of Gold and Silver. Reprinted in U.S. Senate, *International Monetary Conference*. Senate Exec. Doc. No. 58, 45th Congress, 3rd Session. Reprinted by Arno Press, 1979, pp. 558–81.

Jenkinson, C. (Lord Liverpool). 1805. *A Treatise on the Coins of the Realm in a Letter to the King*. London. Reprinted New York: Augustus M. Kelley, 1968.

Jevons, W. 1899. *Money and the Mechanism of Exchange*. London: D. Applegate and Company.

Kenwood, A., and A. Lougheed. 1971. *The Growth of the International Economy, 1820–1960*. London: George Allen and Unwin.

References

Kindleberger, C. 1984. *The Financial History of Western Europe.* London: George Allen and Unwin.

Kydland, F., and E. Prescott. 1977. Rules Rather than Discretion: The Time Inconsistency of Optimal Plans. *Journal of Political Economy*, June: 473–91.

Lane, Frederic C., and Reinhold C. Mueller. 1985. *Money and Banking in Medieval and Renaissance Venice*; Vol. I, *Coins and Moneys of Account.* Baltimore: Johns Hopkins University Press.

Lardy, C. E. 1878. "Statement of the Monetary Legislation and Coinage of Switzerland." Exhibit D 7th Session, Proceedings of the Conference of 1878. Reprinted in United States Senate (1879 [1978]), pp. 190–1.

Laughlin, J. L. 1896. *The History of Bimetallism in the United States.* New York: Appleton.

de Laveleye, E. 1891. *La monnaie et le bimétallisme international.* Paris.

Levasseur, E. 1911. *Histoire du Commerce de la France.* Paris.

Lowndes. 1695. *A Report Containing an Essay for the Amendment of the Silver Coins.* London: Reprinted in McCullough (1856), 1966: 171–258.

Martin, D. A. 1973. "1853: The End of Bimetallism in the United States." *Journal of Economic History* (December): 825–44.

Mayhew, N. 1974. "Numismatic Evidence and Falling Prices in the Fourteenth Century." *Economic History Review*, 2nd ser. 27: 1–15.

1988. *Coinage in France.* London: Seaby.

McCallum, B. 1989. *Monetary Economics: Theory and Policy.* New York: Macmillan Publishing Co.

McCullough, H. R. 1856. *A Select Collection of Scarce and Valuable Tracts on Money.* London: Reprinted New York: Augustus M. Kelley, 1966.

References

McKinnon, R. 1963. Optimum Currency Areas. *American Economic Review*, 53: 717–25.

Mertens, J. E. 1944. *La naissance et le dévéloppement de l'étalonor*. Paris.

Mirabeau. 1790. Mémoire distribué à l'Assemblée Nationale. Paris. Reprinted in Chevalier, *De la baisse probable*, pp. 3–51.

Miskimin, H. 1963. *Money, Prices, and Foreign Exchange in Fourteenth Century France*. New Haven, Conn.: Yale University Press.

 1967. Two reforms of Charlemagne? Weights and Measures in the Middle Ages. *Economic History Review*, 20: 35–52.

 1972. The Enforcement of Gresham's Law. Ms.

de Molinari, G. 1854. De la dépréciation de l'or. *Journal des économistes*, 5: 192–218.

Moore, D. T., and W. A. Oddy. 1985. Touchstones: Some Aspects of Their Nomenclature, Petrography and Provenance. *Journal of Archaeological Science*, 12: 59–80.

Mundell, R. A. 1961. A Theory of Optimal Currency Areas. *American Economic Review*, 51: 637–65.

Munro, J. 1988. Deflation and the Petty Coinage Problem in the Late-Medieval Economy: The Case of Flanders, 1334–1484. *Explorations in Economic History*, 387–423.

Niehans, J. 1978. *The Theory of Money*. Baltimore: Johns Hopkins University Press.

O'Leary, P. 1937. The Coinage Legislation of 1834. *Journal of Political Economy*, XLV: 80–94.

Oppers, S. 1994a. A Model of the Bimetallic System. Ms. University of Michigan. Feb.

 1994b. Arbitrage in bimetallic money supplies: evidence from the exchange rate. Ms. University of Michigan, Mar.

References

Patterson, C. C. 1972. "Silver Stocks and Losses in Ancient and Medieval Times." *Economic History Review*, 25: 205–35.

Peck, C. Wilson. 1960. *English Copper, Tin and Bronze Coins in the British Museum, 1558–1958*. London: The Trustees of the British Museum.

Perkins, Edwin J. 1994. *American Public Finance and Financial Services 1700–1815*. Columbus: Ohio State University Press.

Prestwich, Michael. 1982. The Crown and the Currency: The circulation of money in late 13th and early 14th century England. *Numismatic Chronicle*, 142: 51–65.

Prieur. 1798. Rapport fait au conseil des cinq-cents. Paris. Reprinted in Chevalier, *De la baisse probable*, pp. 52–90.

Rastel, G. 1935. *Les controverses doctrinales sur le bimétallisme*. Paris.

Redish, A. 1984. Why Was Specie Scarce in Colonial Economies? An Analysis of the Canadian Currency, 1796–1830. *Journal of Economic History*, XLIV: 713–28.

1990. The Evolution of the Gold Standard in England. *Journal of Economic History*, 50 (4): 789–805.

1993. The Latin Monetary Union and the Emergence of the International Gold Standard. In M. Bordo and F. Capie, eds., *Monetary Regimes in Transition*. Cambridge: Cambridge University Press, pp. 68–85.

1995. The Persistence of Bimetallism in Nineteenth Century France. *Economic History Review*, XLVIII (4): 717–36.

Remini, R. 1967. *Andrew Jackson and the Bank War*. New York: Norton.

Riley, J., and J. McCusker. 1983. "Money Supply, Economic Growth, and the Quantity Theory of Money: France, 1650–1788." *Explorations in Economic History*, 20: 274–93.

Roberts-Austen, W., and Chandler. 1884. Alloys used for coining.

References

Journal of the Society of Arts, pp. 804–14; 835–47; 881–91; 911–20.

Rochon, A. 1792. *Essai sur les monnaies anciennes et modernes.* Paris. Ms 8^0-3114.

n.d. *Essai sur les monnaies.* Paris. Ms 8^0-37.

Rockoff, H. 1990. The Wizard of Oz as a Monetary Allegory. *Journal of Political Economy*, 98 (4): 739–60.

Rolnick, A., F. Velde, and W. Weber. 1996. The Debasement Puzzle: An Essay on Medieval Monetary History. *Journal of Economic History*, 56: 789–809.

Rolnick, A., and W. Weber. 1986. Gresham's law or Gresham's fallacy? *Journal of Political Economy*, 94: 185–99.

Ruding, R. 1840. *Annals of the coinage of Great Britain*, 2 vols. London.

Russell, H. B. 1898. *International Monetary Conferences.* New York: Harper.

Saint Marc, M. 1983. *Histoire monétaire de la France, 1800–1980.* Paris.

Sargent, T., and B. Smith. 1997. Coinage, Debasements and Gresham's Laws. *Economic Theory*, 10: 197–226.

Sargent, T., and F. Velde. 1998. The Big Problem of Small Change. Ms. University of Chicago.

de Saulcy, F. 1877. *Elements de' histoire des ateliers Monetaires.* Paris.

Say, H. 1843. Du projet de la centralisation de la fabrication des monnaies. *Journal des économistes*, 4: 366–82.

1845. Rejet du projet de loi sur la refonte des monnaies de cuivre et de billon. *Journal des économistes*, 5: 271–75.

Sédillot, René. 1953. *Le franc.* Paris: Recueil Sirey.

Seyd, E. 1879. *The Decline of Prosperity.* London.

Shaw, W. A. 1896. *The History of Currency.* Reprinted 1967. New York: A. M. Kelley.

Snelling, T. 1766. A View of the Copper Coin and Coinage of England. London.

References

Soetbeer, A. 1879. *Edelmetall-Produktion und Verthvehdltneiss swischen geld und silber.* Gotha J. Perthes.

Spooner, F. 1972. *The International Economy and Monetary Movements in France, 1493–1725.* Cambridge, Mass.: Harvard University Press.

Spufford, Peter. 1986. *Handbook of Medieval Exchange.* London: Royal Historical Society.

1988. *Money and Its Use in Medieval Europe.* Cambridge: Cambridge University Press.

Supple, B. 1957. Currency and Commerce in the Early Seventeenth Century. *Economic History Review*, 10: 239–55.

Sussman, N. 1993. Debasements, Royal Revenues, and Inflation in France during the Hundred Years' War, 1415–22. *Journal of Economic History*, 53: 44–70.

1998. The Late Medieval Bullion Famine Reconsidered. *Journal of Economic History*, 58: 126–54.

Taxay, D. 1966. *The U.S. Mint and Coinage.* New York: Arco Publishing Co.

Temin, P. 1975. *The Jacksonian Economy.* New York: Norton.

Thuillier, G. 1983. *La Monnaie en France.* Paris.

United States Senate. 1879 [1978]. *International Monetary Conference of 1878, Proceedings and Exhibits.* Reprinted New York: Arno Press.

Usher, A. P. 1957. Machines and Mechanisms. In C. Singer, E. J. Holmyard, A. R. Hall and Trevor Williams, eds., *A History of Technology*, Vol. 3, Oxford University Press, pp. 324–46.

Van der Wee, H. 1977. Monetary, Credit and Banking Systems. In E. E. Rich and C. H. Wilson, eds., *The Cambridge Economic History of Europe*, Vol. 5. Cambridge: Cambridge University Press, pp. 290–393.

Van Werveke, Hans. 1934. Monnaie de compte et monnaie reelle. *Revue belge de philologie et d'histoire*, 13: 123–52.

References

Vaughan, R. 1675. *A Discourse of Coin and Coinage, Etc.* London: Reprinted McCullough (1856), 1966, pp. 1–118.

Velde, R., W. Weber, and R. Wright. 1996. A Model of Commodity Money, with Applications to Gresham's Law and the Debasement Puzzle. Federal Reserve Bank of Minneapolis, Staff Report 215.

de Wailly, N. 1857. *Memoire sur les Variations de la livre Tournois depuis la règne de Saint Louis jusqu'a l'établissment de la monnaie décimale.* Paris: Imprimerie Imperial.

White, J. 1830. Letter to Hon. S. D. Ingham, on the Relative Value of Gold and Silver. Reprinted in U.S. Senate, *International Monetary Conference*, Senate Exec. Doc. No. 58, 45th Congress, 3rd Session. Reprinted by Arno Press, 1979, pp. 655–62.

Willis, H. P. 1901. *A History of the Latin Monetary Union.* Chicago.

Yeager, L. 1976. *International Monetary Relations.* New York: Harper and Row.

Index

Index

Law, John, 73, 82, 86
Le Blanc, F., 58–9
Liverpool (earls of)
  see Jenkinson, Charles (1st
    earl of Liverpool);
    Jenkinson, Robert B. (2d
    earl of Liverpool)
LMU
  see Latin Monetary Union
    (LMU)
Lowndes, William (British
    Secretary of the
    Treasury), 107n1
Lowndes, William (U. S.
    House of
    Representatives), 217

McCallum, B., 243
McCusker, J., 71n17
Malynes, Gerald, 116
Martin, D. A., 232, 234
Mayhew, N., 47–8, 132–33
medium of exchange
  need for multiple
    denominations, 15
  separate from unit of
    account, 8
Mestrell, Eloi, 57
mint equivalent
  defined, 27
  gold and silver, England,
    44, 49, 89–92
  gold and silver, France, 44,
    49–51, 93–103

mint price
  defined, 27
  in England and France
    (1360–1789), 52–3
  relation to seignorage rate,
    71
mint ratio
  early modern England,
    51
  early modern France, 51
  estimates, 1700–1880,
    227
  U. S. revision of 1834,
    223
mint technology
  hammering, 54
  rolling presses, 56
  screw presses, 56–7
  and the transition to the
    gold standard, 4, 10
mint technology, England
  Boulton's mint, 154–5
  touted advantages of
    Boulton and Watt's press,
    144
mint technology, France
  mechanization, 178–9
  rejection of Boulton's
    press, 175
mint technology, U. S.
  horses vs. steam engines in
    the U. S., 225
  introduction of steam in
    1830s, 226

272

Continued from series information page

The Strategy and
Consistency of
Federal Reserve Monetary
Policy, 1924–1933
David C. Wheelock
0-521-39155-5

Banking Panics of the
Great Depression
Elmus Wicker
0-521-663466

Monetary Regimes in
Transition
Michael D. Bordo and
Forrest Capie, Editors
0-521-41906-9

Canada and the
Gold Standard
Trevor J. O. Dick and John
E. Floyd
0-521-40408-8

Elusive Stability
Barry Eichengreen
0-521-44847-6

Europe's Postwar Recovery
Barry Eichengreen
0-521-48279-8

A Monetary History
of Italy
Michele Fratianni and
Franco Spinelli
0-521-44315-6

The Economics of
World War II
Mark Harrison, editor
0-521-620465

Managing the
Franc Poincaré
Kenneth Moure
0-521-39458-9

The Rise of
Financial Capitalism
Larry Neal
0-521-45738-6

Between the
Dollar–Sterling Gold
Points
Lawrence H. Officer
0-521-4546-2

The Credit–Anstalt Crisis
of 1931
Aurel Schubert
0-521-36537-6

The Gold Standard and
Related Regimes
Michael D. Bordo
0-521-55006-8